THE COLOR OF GOD

THE COLOR OF GOD

The Concept of God
in Afro-American Thought

by
MAJOR J. JONES

MERCER

ISBN 0-86554-274-0 {CASEBOUND}
ISBN 0-86554-276-7 {PAPERBACK}

The paper used in this publication meets
the minimum requirements of American National Standard
for Information Sciences—Permanence of Paper
for Printed Library Materials, ANSI Z39.48-1984.

Library of Congress Cataloging-in-Publication Data
Jones, Major J., 1918–
The color of God:
the concept of God in Afro-American thought
Includes index.
1. God.   2. God—History of doctrines.   3. Black theology.
4. Afro-Americans—Religion.   5. United States—Religion.
I. Title.
BT102.J647   1987
231'.08996073—dc19   87-184449

CONTENTS

To
MATTIE
And
CHANDRA

PREFACE

Sometimes the bookshelf reveals as many gaps as bindings. As a writer, I am under the conviction that a vital area lies unexplored: Black Theology is a fit and necessary, although still largely underexplored and rather new, subject of theological discourse. With this book, I would hope to subtract from the world's sum of spiritual illiteracy by adding to the growing body of Black Theology as part of the total body of Christian thought. Black Theology comprehends deeply the Black experience of Christianity: at its highest, Black Theology transcends all color.

More than fifty Black scholars at the October 1981 meeting of the Society for the Study of Black Religion, teachers in college, university, and theological communities, expressed a critical and urgent need for broader publications on Black religious thought. The question that demanded an answer was: "Why is there not more Black Christian Theology available?" Many members felt that the literature of Black Theology needed to be broader in scope and updated. At other, similar meetings of Black scholars, where teaching needs for an expanding quantity of literature on Black Theology were expressed, and at the 1983 Annual Meeting of the Society of Christian Ethics, where White and Black teachers in many academic communities reiterated their frustration at the paltry number of published offerings in Black Theology, Black theologians especially were conscious of the neglect of Black Theology as a teaching resource. This book is a response to that question and these needs so urgently voiced.

Out of a long and difficult process and after many revisions, this book issues forth partly as my personal view of God, the faith stance of one who was born and reared within the tradition of the Black Church and who by work, study, and profession became a "sometime theologian." As an assessment of the status of the God-concept within the Black community of faith, this book is not the result of a survey taken of what others have thought and say about God. Nonetheless, I am in conversation with current "God talk" and have been particularly illuminated by reflections of God in the glass of Black Theology. I have culled from current expressions of Black Theology what I understand to be a uniquely Black concept of God, a God-concept developed from the history of a particular people who have struggled, not only for physical freedom but also for the preservation of both their freedom of mind and their sense of authentic humanity. This Afro-Americanized concept of God developed within the unique, Black religious experience of an oppressed people; as such, it could not be contained within the God-concept of the White people who had been cast in the painful and limiting role of oppressors.

To recognize the importance of this Black God-conceptual distinction, one first must recognize and concede that the Afro-American religious experience itself is not clear or separate or even identifiable in the minds of many well-intentioned, deeply religious, Black Christians from the mainly White culture in which they live. This unclarity exists because Black people too often do not recognize that their White Christian brothers and sisters worship a God who is essentially White. This White God-concept has allowed many White people to remain comfortably unconcerned about the oppression that Black people and their God suffer from a racist society ordered and determined by White people and their God. Black consciousness, indeed, demands liberation and purification of the God-concept itself. We will free it from the many alien connotations that deny the full affirmation of Black humanity, merely because one is Black and not White.

No Black person, I hold, can see God in clear perspective and not eventually confront the deep questions of personhood related to being Black and living in White America. No one—whatever their color—can see God authentically without facing the deepest questions of personal humanity sooner or later. One cannot divide or separate Black people's being Black from their being human. Those who have failed to see that in Black people blackness and humanity are one have also failed to face the White reality of a host culture, which has traditionally denied Black people their humanity for no reason other than their color.

Since 1619 and too often, Black Afro-Americans have had to cope with a Western concept of God which implied that God is White. Without a clear, Black God-concept, stripped of White connotations, a Black person is not free to worship or affirm God as one with whom that Black person can completely identify. By manipulating the White God-concept, many White people have sought to control Black people's thinking, even to the point of setting them against their own blackness. As James N. Evans puts it, the ultimate aim of the White oppressor is to force Black people "either to give up their blackness for the sake of their humanity or sacrifice their humanity for the sake of their blackness."[1] If one

---

[1] James N. Evans, "Apartheid as Idolatry," *Christianity and Crisis* 41:20 (14 December 1981): 347ff.

cannot free God of alien connotations, then one cannot affirm one's personal, full humanity. To be free of the ex-master the former slave must cease to embrace the master's highest symbol of identification: the slaveholder's God. Does it not always follow that the inner subjectivity of Afro-American people, of which their blackness is an inseparable part, is a source of the deepest possible truth about themselves and their God?[2] The extent to which their God is free of alien connotations is the measure of that people's freedom.

In this book I have sought to express a true and authentic Afro-Americanized concept of God. This God-concept can best reveal itself to minds free of alien distortions that becloud God's efforts at self-disclosure to a people in the relevance of their particular existence. If we, both Black and White Christians, concede that the mind is God's highest created gift, then it is our God-given duty to keep it free and pure of alien attempts to control it. The late Steve Biko of South Africa was right in reminding us that "the most potent weapon in the hands of the oppressor is the mind of the oppressed."[3] Especially the concept of God, when it is alien, can hold one, mind and body, in bondage to a distorted understanding of one's own true selfhood, one's own humanity, and in the case of Black people, the meaning of one's own blackness. Any adequate study of the history of faith in God in the Black community ought to find that God's ontological being had been Afro-Americanized. I address this book to a people in whose deeper understanding I have found this God-concept.

In the first part, I relate the concept of God to the African and Afro-American cultural contexts. These two divergent histories have flowed together in the Black Afro-American concept of God, and they have carried that God-concept into the liberation struggle. In the other part of the book, I develop a new frame of reference for understanding a transcendent God removed from the stifling limits of White-only concepts. Black Theology has missed its calling if it cannot develop anew and maintain a total intellectual offensive at least against all color-distorted concepts of God—while avoiding similar distortions of its own. No God-concept is universally adequate for all peoples. Too much God-reality has been expressed from the narrow point of view of White theologians who live in Europe and the Americas. Black people of faith must now abandon the partial frames of alien reference imposed on them and seek fresh and new God-concepts that will free them for a new creation. This explosion of freedom must first be our gift to ourselves and then our gift to all Christians and the world.

---

[2]Ibid.

[3]Ibid.

By the God-concept expressed in these pages, I contend that God is One Unitary Holy Personal Being according to the tradition of the Trinity, who exists in three modes of divine being: Father, Son, and Holy Spirit. The Unity of the three holds in the Being of God as Father, God as Son, and God as Holy Spirit; and all three are One as our Creator, our Reconciler and Redeemer, and our Personal Agent. God is thus one and undivided in operation as well as in essence.

The Black Theologian—let it be said—must be an iconoclast of his or her own justifications, reductions, and accommodations, lest we commit the equal and opposite idolatry of White Theology. Black Theology, theological feminism, and any other liberation theology or any human ideological captivity of God's purity and freedom can be as much a distortion of God as the White God of oppression has been, rendering God less than God, creating God in the human image rather than the other way around. To make the God-concept pure is to free it and lift it up, so that it may transcend all narrow, merely human points of view.

Faithfulness to the Holy Trinity is one motivation underlying this book; faithfulness to my human color is the other. I urgently desire to redeem the term "black" from prior negative connotations. I relate "blackness" to the God-concept in such a way as to make the word God-given, a positive ontological affirmation. If God makes himself known to each person in the unilateral relevancy of his or her existential being and if that person is Black, then God relates to those people through their Black human being. Moving between these two poles of theological premise—the Trinity and blackness—I have developed my Afro-Americanized concept of God. It is my attempt to see God through the eyes of a people to whom God has been made known in the light of their particular history. By seeing God reflected to us in this glass darkly then, we sense no problem with being Black under God.

Should my Black and White sisters find these pages not fully free of sexist language, I ask them to forgive me for being a male theologian. I was made more aware of this traditional weakness in language and expression by Susan Brooks Thistlewaite's *God's Fierce Whimsey: Christian Feminism and Theological Education,*—a perceptive review of the Mudflower Collective, seven women who are theological educators or administrators attempting to convey something of what it means to relate to God as a woman and understand that relationship. In the chapter on "God-Stories," Beverly Wildung Harrison of Union Theological Seminary (New York) puts the God-human relation in femaleness this way: "God is wherever there is real desire, real longing, for connection. . . . God is in the connection." It is possible to tell God's story "because we told our stories of race and class first. God's life is not over, beyond, or in spite of the life of the world."[4] This "life" of God in the world—which is the emphasis of the book—brings God close enough to relate to each person in his maleness or her femaleness while continuing to transcend the mere level of the human.

Finally, any work of this sort would be impossible without a sense of the lively support of an aware academic community—people who help in both open and unrecognized ways, and who nurture one's intellectual growth through exchange and challenge. Beyond the Interdenominational Theological Center and the larger Atlanta University Center, I have been deeply influenced by The Society for the Study of Black Religion, the Society of Christian Ethics, and former students and friends in the Black Church, contact with whom has made my life rich.

A special word of thanks goes to those who worked so hard to prepare the final manuscript. I thank and acknowledge authors and publishers who permitted their works to be quoted by naming them in the footnotes. A personal word of thanks is extended to the people of Mercer University Press for their help in making this publication possible.

Major J. Jones
The Atlanta University Center
Robert W. Woodruff Library

---

[4]Susan Brooks Thistlewaite, "Together in Difference," *Christianity and Crisis* 46:11 (11 August 1986): 277-80. A review of *God's Fierce Whimsey: Christian Feminism and Theological Education* by the Mudflower Collective (New York: Pilgrim Press, 1985).

CHAPTER ONE

Black Theology
in Historical Perspective

WHY A BLACK THEOLOGY?

After so much has been written expressive of Black Theology, it surprises
one to hear so many people still questioning the need for Black Theology. Such
a question sounds still stranger if one accepts the basic assumption that a theological system should satisfy at least the two following basic needs: First, a
theological system should be a statement of the truth of the Christian message
and the interpretation of that truth for the whole community of faith. Second,
a theological system should be a particular statement reflecting the need of
people experiencing different cultural contexts for particular theologies that
speak directly to their temporal situations. In this sense, Black Theology is a
particular interpretation of the general Christian message for the Black community of faith. It is not a message separate from and totally apart; rather, it
is a necessary part of the total theologizing process. Indeed, void of a Black
theological dimension, the whole theologizing process pales to anemic incom-
pleteness and inadequacy. In the larger sense, a Black theological statement
embraces both the Black and White communities of faith.

If theology's primary aim is to render intelligible the meaning of God's
action in the world to all people, then the theological and ethical interpretations of the religious experiences of a community of faith must take new forms
in every new age or different cultural context. The meaning of the Christian
faith must be reexamined existentially in each new historical setting, interpreting the ever-changing thought patterns and experiences of believers. This
task of relational interpretation and reinterpretation, testing and retesting, has
been performed whenever those who loved God deeply and who took Christianity seriously, held it worthy of a critical examination and new assessment.

The Black theologian's task must encompass the responsibility of deriving a systematic, critical evaluation and a rational defense of what has been interpreted as the central meaning of the Christian faith. This central meaning must then translate into both personal and collective commitments and subsequent meaningful actions. Therefore, a systematic theology for Blacks is a theoretical discipline that discovers, expounds, and defends the truths implied in the experience of the Christian Black community.

The Black theologian's data embrace the Bible, the history of the Christian faith, and the sum total of the oral and written experiences of Black people. The cultural roots of Black Theology grow in the written and oral traditions of human struggle set forth in song, story, sermons, and all of life's remembered experiences.

This working definition of black systematic theology in general leads us to the particular need for a Black Theology. An authentic, legitimate, and necessary Black Theology has always existed; however, Black Theology has been heretofore overlooked, because White Theology has traditionally excluded the Black religious experience. But very few contemporary White theologians give written evidence that they have read even a respectable selection of the current literature of Black Theology. Perhaps this is because they feel it not to be of educational importance. Whether White theologians read it or not, Black scholars need to insist on the development of the growing literature interpreting Black Theology.

WHAT IS BLACK THEOLOGY?

To summarize: Black Theology is a conscience-inspired effort to interpret the Christian message for the Black community of faith. Black Theology has always been a necessary part of the life and spirit of the Black Church since before the Civil War. The current Black Theology movement began in the 1960s, when Black theologians acquired a new existential mood. They recognized the task of relating the experiences of Black Christians to the corpus of Christian theology. The Black theological frame of reference became a recognizable theological entity first in the works of James H. Cone and has been a close relative of the Black Studies movement in America. Arresting questions raised by Cone and in the works of many other Black scholars persist.[1] Gayraud S. Wilmore, as he so often has done, puts Black Theology in its rightful place when he contends that

> Black theology is not an unsophisticated, anti-intellectual reaction to whatever is happening at any moment in time—a mixture of emotion and pious

---

[1]James H. Cone, *Black Theology and Black Power* (New York: Seabury Press, 1969).

propaganda. It is, rather, a hardheaded, practical, and passionate reading of the signs of the times in the white community as well as the black. It is an elucidation of what we have understood God to be about in our history, particularly in the history of our struggle against racial oppression. . . . Black theology was formulated by Christian activists in response to events—events which had the unmistakable sign that God is saying and doing something about black people in white America.[2]

Black theology is not separate and apart from other Christian theologies; it is rather a necessary and inseparable part of the total theological undertaking. There can therefore be no wholeness to the theological discipline without a Black theological dimension. Professor Geddes Hanson of Princeton University rightly contends that

Black theology brings its reflection on the Black Experience to the theological conference table claiming itself to be the salt without which any attempt to do theological business in America today is without savor.

Implicit in the previous remarks are the assumptions that Black Theology, in doing its job well, will force Protestant thought to the point of reconsidering its eschatology and its anthropology. It must, in fact, do more.[3]

If, then, Black Theology is to speak realistically for and cogently to Black people whose lives have been worn down, defeated, and forgotten, it must first be able to reclaim that people from the humiliation and shame of being Black within the context of a pro-White culture. Hanson furhter contends:

Black Theology . . . is a self-conscious effort to relate the experience of American Blackness to the corpus of Christian theology. Proceeding from the conviction that theology itself is the attempt to deal with the realities of human experience from the perspective of the divine-human negotiation, Black Theology lifts up the reality of the experience of Blackness in America as being relevant to the theological task.[4]

Black Theology thus has a unique and necessary mission in the life of the Black Church. Its broad task makes it belong specially to a people who had been assigned a lowly place in the context of American life. Black people had long needed a formal Black Theology; the current Black Theology movement has given them a written religious expression derived from their history.

---

[2]G. S. Wilmore and James H. Cone, *Black Theology: A Documentary History* (Maryknoll NY: Orbis Books, 1979) 4.

[3]Geddes Hanson, "Black Theology and Protestant Thought," *Social Progress: A Journal of Church and Society* (September/ October 1969): 10.

[4]Ibid., 6.

Black Theology—like all theologies arises from a people's common experiences of God. At this moment in history, the Black community must express itself theologically from a Black frame of reference in language that speaks directly to the current conditions of Black people.

The Committee on Theological Perspectives of the National Committee of Black Churchmen expressed in clear language this opinion:

> Black Theology is not a gift of the Christian gospel dispensed to slaves; it is, rather, an appropriation which the slaves made of the gospel given by their White oppressors.
>
> Black Theology is a theology of Black Liberation. It seeks to plumb the Black condition in the light of God's revelation in Jesus Christ, so that the Black community can see the gospel is commensurate with the achievement of Black humanity. Black Theology is a theology of "blackness." It is the affirmation of Black humanity that emancipates Black people in that it says "no" to the encroachment of White oppression.[5]

Black Theology is therefore especially helpful in interpreting the inner conflicts that the Black experience has effected within the inner being of the Black person. Black Theology gives new meaning to the concept of blackness as it seeks to relate blackness to a liberating truth. As James H. Cone observes,

> The central question that gave birth to black theology was: "What has the gospel of Jesus to do with the oppressed black people's struggle for justice in American society?" The radical black NCBC clergy pursued a substantial examination of that question, which separated them from both white liberal and black conservative church persons. In the process of rereading the Bible in the light of black history, black clergy radicals . . . began to refer to God as the liberator of the oppressed Hebrew slaves in Egypt and to Jesus as the new liberator whom God has anointed "to preach the good news to the poor, to proclaim release to the captives, and to set at liberty those who are oppressed." (Luke 4: 18-19, RSV)[6]

Thus, in current times, Black Theology expresses a new light of freedom under God. Having tasted that freedom through identification with God's intention for Black humanity, the Black person, locked in the struggle for lib-

---

[5]A statement of the National Committee of Black Churchmen produced by the Committee on Theological Perspectives, issued 13 June, 1966, at the Interdenominational Theological Center in Atlanta, Georgia.

[6]James H. Cone, *For My People: Black Theology and the Black Church* (Maryknoll NY: Orbis Books, 1984) 80.

eration, will stop at nothing short of expressing both in act and being an ever stronger affirmation of Black selfhood. Black Theology often becomes that truth which places a Black person for the first time in touch with a deep core-self which is the real human self; and once a person finds that core meaning of selfhood, he or she is prepared to give all for it. This is the ultimate liberation intent of Black Theology.

If the German "theologian of hope" Jürgen Moltmann is right in saying that the "gospel of Christ frees a man to be for those who labor and are heavily laden, the humiliated and abused,"[7] then it would seem that Black Theology represents an important and necessary facet of the gospel message that Jesus brought to the world. In this sense, Black Theology is but one important facet of a many-sided application of the gospel to the current issues of our time.

Black Theology thus puts Black self-identity into a contemporary theological context that is part of the total, authentically human quest; as such, it is consistent with the gospel of Jesus Christ. The current existential mood of Black theological reflection stems from the recognition that Black self-identity can best be defined from a Black theological frame of reference. Because Black people have never been fully accepted in America, and because they are still treated as the "other Americans," the Black theological task becomes all the more necessary. James Baldwin saw the problem clearly when he wrote:

> I was a kind of bastard of the West; when I followed my past, I did not find myself in Europe, but in Africa. And this meant that in some subtle way, in a really profound way, I brought to Shakespeare, Bach, Rembrandt, to the stones of Paris, to the Cathedral at Chartres, and to the Empire State Building, a special attitude. These were really not my creations, they did not contain my history. I might search them in vain forever for any reflection of myself.[8]

Black Theology aims at making sense out of the Black experience for those pilgrims who have passed or are yet passing through the ordeal. It seeks to illuminate both the faith content and the nature of Black existence, so that those who experience it can relate to God in more meaningful ways.

THE SCOPE OF BLACK THEOLOGY

Black Theology is both historical and systematic in its approach; yet, the content has necessarily not been as broad as theology's in general. This is because it confines itself to the concerns of the Black experience. Thus, all the

---

[7]Jürgen Moltmann, "Toward a Political Hermeneutics of the Gospel," *Union Seminary Quarterly Review,* Summary (1968): 313-14.

[8]James Baldwin, *Notes of a Native Son* (New York: Beacon Press, 1955) 6-7.

general themes of traditional systematic theology do not appear in what is currently labeled Black Theology. Generally speaking, Black theologians have been preoccupied with central religious themes that relate to Black self-identity, power, revolution, and liberation.

Many other Black theological topics correspond to general theological themes and do not exist apart from them. Generally speaking, however, Black Theology has not been a systematic theology simply because Black theologians have not yet addressed themselves to the total content of systematic theology. Black theologians have meant their theology to be a positive interpretation of the meaning of blackness in the light of contemporary events. This does not mean, however, that other themes are not important; rather, it means that there are still many other themes yet to be addressed by Black Theology.

THE TASKS OF BLACK THEOLOGY

First, Black Theology has been and continues to be primarily a theology of protest. Its province has been the expression of a deep dissatisfaction felt by Blacks with their conditions in a pro-White culture. It is a theological protest that attempts to express what Black theologians think—namely, that theology in general should also be protesting the evil treatment of a community of God's people in America, but has failed to protest.

Second, Black Theology calls for a more radical and complete revolutionary change. Most current Black theologians insist that to change the plight of Blacks within the context of American culture will take nothing short of a radical revolution. Whether or not such a revolution is violent is not the primary concern of many Black theologians. Change alone is the concern. The call is for an unconditional commitment to change.

Third, Black Theology is a theology of liberation seeking to free Black people from the inner bondage of their own thoughts concerning blackness. Black Theology aims to inspire in Blacks a sense of worth, self-esteem, and "at-homeness" within their own subjective blackness.

Fourth, Black Theology strives to make Black people more humane in their feelings, attitudes, and ultimate human objectives.

Fifth, one aim of Black liberation according to Black Theology, is freedom for Black people from their traditional fear of Whites, so that they not only can articulate their feelings but also so that they will act upon them.

Sixth, Black Theology holds that to be a person is to act like a person within any human context. This is the ultimate aim of Black Theology. Black people must feel that they are completely capable and fit to live full lives under God and in relation to all God's children. God is no respecter of persons, and neither should his children be. Black Theology generates within Black people the strength needed to resist the forces that threaten their humanity and that attempt to reduce them to an inhuman status less than that of a child of God.

Finally, Black Theology links God's power to the Black person's own inner prevailing strength. This inner prevailing strength allows Black persons to live within the pro-White world without hate or bitterness, but with a sense of self-worth. This is the ultimate, liberating gift of Black Theology.

BLACK THEOLOGY AND THE CONCEPT OF BLACKNESS

To speak knowledgeably of the contemporary Black religious experience is to relate it to the current Black consciousness movement. This relational understanding grasps "blackness" as an important facet of the wholeness of life in the Black frame of reference. Whether in Black history, Black Theology, or some other refraction of the prism of current Black expression, an adequate Black self-understanding does not emerge until Black people fully recognize and accept their blackness as essential to the true sense of their authentic humanity. Allan A. Boesak, a leading South African Black theologian, instructs us that: ". . . Blackness is a reality that embraces the totality of Black existence."[9]

Recognition of one's blackness is an affirmation of one's very being. Full acceptance of one's blackness is an experience similar to spiritual rebirth or total conversion, and it frees one for full participation in the creation of a new humanity. This full awareness of one's blackness is one of the central aims of the Black Theology movement. Whoever misunderstands this aim of the Black Theology movement, that "Blackness is an awareness, . . . an attitude, and . . . a state of mind," will also misunderstand the moral muscle of the movement: To affirm and assert one's blackness is a "bold and serious determination to be a person in one's own right."[10]

Not to embrace and assert one's blackness is not to embrace one's true self, one's true existence as a human person. Indeed, to reject the fact of one's blackness is to reject what it means to be Black, and to invite the observation that one is strange and "other." It is to deny that one is human.

Winthrop D. Jackson relates how blackness, as color, initially struck the perceptions of the English who first encountered Black people in Africa in 1631:

The most arresting characteristic of the new[ly] discovered African was his

---

[9]Allan Aubrey Boesak, *Farewell to Innocence: A Socio-Ethical Study on Black Theology and Black Power* (Maryknoll NY: Orbis Books, 1977) 26-27

[10]Ibid.

color. Travelers rarely failed to comment upon it; indeed, when describing Negroes they frequently began with complexion and moved on to dress . . . and manners. Even more sympathetic observers seemed to find blackness a most salient quality in Negroes; "although the people were black and naked, yet they were civil."[11]

In the eyes of "others," Black people are strange for the simple reason of their color. To be perceived as a black person is to be set aside often as a non-human other. Complexion and complexion alone has had a powerful impact on Black/White perceptions and, therefore, relations. White people frequently seem unable to penetrate color conceptually to the point of accepting the authentic humanity of Black people. To be unable to see a person beyond color is to be unable to afford that person the equality of being and personhood. By taking the problems inherent in blackness seriously, Black Theology attempts to restore personhood to a Black frame of reference.

In a positive sense, Black Theology is a situational theology. Boesak contends that it aids Black people in their "attempt to come to terms theologically" with their status in the context of society. Black Theology seeks to interpret the gospel so that the situation of Black people will begin to make sense. The great psychological benefit of Black Theology is its assertion of what Black people have learned the hard way—that a person incapable of powerful self-affirmation in spite of the anxiety of "non-being" is forced into a weak and reduced self-affirmation. Boesak further asserts that Black Theology

> . . . seeks to take seriously the biblical emphasis on the wholeness of life, which has always had its counterpart in the African heritage, trying to transform that departmentalized theology Blacks have inherited from the Western world into a biblical holistic theology. It is part of the Black struggle towards liberation from religious, economic, psychological, and cultural dependency.[12]

Like Boesak, James Cone correctly argues that Black Theology is an authentic expression of Christian theology, arising from the tradition of Black struggle for liberation, equal justice, and human dignity. But Cone's reasoning falters when he states his case with an absolute one-sidedness: "First, there can be no theology of the gospel which does not arise from an oppressed community."[13]

Although Black Theology is a reflecting upon the religious nature of Black people's struggle in a society where that struggle is no part of White Chris-

---

[11]Winthrop D. Jackson, *White over Black: American Attitudes toward the Negro, 1550-1812* (Chapel Hill: University of North Carolina Press, 1968) 4-7.

[12]Boesak, *Farewell to Innocence,* 13.

[13]Cone, *Black Theology and Black Power,* 31ff.

tians' everyday experience, Black Theology seeks in no way to be less than a wholly Christian theology. The gospel in focus must speak to the oppressor as well as to the oppressed; for, God speaks to both. Otherwise Amos's message to the oppressor would have lost its cogency. And Isaiah—himself a member of the elite in Israel—would have found no ears to hear the powerful message he was given.

Cone rightly contends that "Black Theology is a facet of Christian Theology because it centers in God's actions in the world."[14] Further, he states: "There is only one principle which guides the thinking and action of Black Theology: an unqualified commitment of the Black community as that community seeks to define its existence in the light of God's liberating work in the world. This means that Black Theology refuses to be guided by ideas and concepts alien to black people."[15]

Black Theology has contributed to the mature thinking of Black people, helping them accept blackness as a positive given. At one with the Black awareness movement in acceptance of this givenness, Black Theology reinforces an independent affirmation of black selfhood that must be respected. Having acquired the independence of selfhood, many Black people now accept no exceptions. Increasingly, as a result of the emphasis on blackness and in spite of heavy external odds negating Black selfhood, more and more Black people have acquired the radical courage to be. Their courage expresses itself in a growing tendency to assert themselves ontologically at the forward edge of becoming more and more a new Black people.

To be liberated is to become conscious of the real self, the very inner core of being. Once one find's one's true identity, one that is totally unrelated to what others may have thought or falsely defined it to be—one has become a liberated, free person. This is the sense in which Black Theology is a new theological expression of a fresh and indigenous message of liberation, freedom, and ultimate salvation in the new light of blackness.

This innovative way of thinking, moreover, has effected a radical change in how Black people now view Black existence under God by motivating them to become aware of traditional African religious thought and African concepts of God. The agenda of Black Theology to Afro-American Black religious thought and experience to traditional Black Christianity is discussed below.

The central aim of Black Theology espoused in these pages is to make the Christian faith more intelligible to Black people by contributing to their re-

---

[14]Ibid.

[15]James H. Cone, *A Black Theology of Liberation* (Philadelphia: J. B. Lippincott Company, 1970) 33.

ligious understanding of the struggle for Black self-affirmation, self-determination, and the courage to become what God wills for all human beings.
The literature currently labeled "Black Theology" had its origins in a felt need
to interpret the spiritual dimensions of Black people's self-awareness. As the
theological expression of the Black consciousness movement, Black Theology
is aimed at giving a radical and timely reinterpretation of the meaning of
blackness. One cannot understand any facet of the movement toward Black
awareness without realizing that, as never before, many Black people have come
to understand the givenness in blackness in the fact that we are born Black;
no other choice is open to us.[16] Heretofore, we sought to escape our blackness.
But now, history and current Black conditions have brought us to an acceptance of our rootedness in blackness. Above all, the Black awareness movement has moved Black people to an independent thought stance and, therefore,
to a new level of freedom. For the first time, in American history, Black people are compelled to articulate deeply, openly, and authentically how they feel
without any hesitations about what others may think. Black Theology is the
theological voice in this new climate of free expression. For these reasons,
blackness has become a central facet of current Christian theological expression.

BLACK HISTORY AND BLACK THEOLOGY:
AFRICAN RELIGIOUS ROOTS

The history of American Black religious experience is Afro-American, and it
must be understood in this narrow and special light. Although the first Black
people were landed in America in 1619, Christian denominations in the South
did not move to Christianize Blacks until almost two hundred years later. Henry
H. Mitchell observed that: "By this time the most White Christians could do
was to superimpose their formality on a faith that had acquired and maintained
its own Afro-Christian character underground."[17] The accommodation of the
Christian message by Black people in America was similar to its reception by African peoples in their native Africa. John Mbiti states: "The Christian message,
on coming to African peoples, found a well-established notion that God rescues
people even when all help is exhausted, and that this rescue is primarily from
material and physical dangers which confront the individual and the commu-

---

[16]Deotis Roberts, "Black Consciousness in Theological Perspective," in *Quest for
a Black Theology,* ed. James J. Gardner and J. Deotis Roberts (Philadelphia: Pilgrim
Press, 1971) 62ff.

[17]Henry H. Mitchell, *Black Belief: Folk Beliefs of Blacks in America and West Africa*
(New York: Harper & Row, 1975) 15.

nity."[18] Africans, Mbiti observes, made two general responses to the message of Christianity. The first response was that: "Africans would reject it if it did not penetrate into those areas which, in their experience, called for salvation." The second response was that "Africans could" accept the gospel and force it to fit into whatever needed 'redemptive application.' "[19]

As Gayraud S. Wilmore described them, African religions "are not mere[ly] crude and unenlightened superstitions, but they are mature, enlightened beliefs and practices common to many religions and similar in many ways to contemporary Christian faith."[20] The reasoning of Mbiti and Wilmore leads one to conclude that the Afro-American understanding of the gospel from the very beginning was predicated on those Black people's own terms. Blacks heard the gospel message and learned the teachings of Jesus as a biblical declaration of their liberation and freedom both as individuals and as a people. Certainly, this was no part of the understanding of the gospel in the intentions of the White preachers. But more than anything else, by looking "from within," at the levels of religion that Wilmore calls "unconscious," Black people both in America and Africa heard the true meaning of the gospel. Black religious experience is the repository where the African religious heritage was held in trust below the conscious surface, out of sight of the slave masters who sought to stamp out every aspect of the Black people's past, thereby to reduce them to the status of a more truly "slave people." But that hyphenation of Black African religion and the Christian gospel as heard by Blacks in America would give rise to Afro-American Black Christian radicalism. Henry H. Mitchell summarizes the Afro-American connection this way:

> The ideological basis for the thoroughly religious conviction that the African High God was opposed to American-style slavery was wholly independent of the high religion of Whites. Blacks later sought and easily found biblical proof texts for their conviction about slavery. The most obvious text was the Exodus story of the divine deliverance of the Jews from Egypt. "Let my people go," said a Negro spiritual. But the human gospel of dignity and freedom crossed over from Africa with the slaves, and it never died.[21]

---

[18]John Mbiti, "Our Saviour as an African Experience," in *Christ and Spirit,* ed. S. S. Salley and B. Lindars (Cambridge MA: Cambridge University Press, 1973) 397-414.

[19]Ibid.

[20]Gayraud S. Wilmore, *Black Religion and Black Radicalism* (Garden City NY: Doubleday and Company, 1972) 22.

[21]Mitchell, *Black Belief,* 33.

The African's "redemptive application" of the Christian gospel—to use Mbiti's phrase—is the adaptive quality to be seen throughout the whole of the African religious encounter with Christianity. That peculiar utilization of the Christian gospel made the difference in the "decolonized" African understanding of the Christian message on the one hand and the traditional understanding of the Christian message among American Blacks on the other. When African and American Black scholars first talked, this difference was not so clearly recognized as it subsequently came to be, and the contrast was sharp between the two groups of thinkers.[22]

However, in both the African and the Afro-American encounters with Christianity, we now know that a similar process of "redemptive application" of the gospel was taking place, if at an "unconscious" level or below the surface, on the western side of the Atlantic as well. The results in Africa and the results in America have been the same. I agree with Wilmore, who asserts that "Blacks have used Christianity not as it was delivered to them by segregated White churches, but as its truth was authenticated to them in the experience of suffering, to reinforce an ingrained religious temperament and to produce an indigenous religion oriented to freedom and human welfare."[23]

BLACK HISTORY AND BLACK THEOLOGY: AFRO-AMERICAN RELIGIOUS ROOTS

The history of Black people in America is entirely different from that of White America or any other ethnic group. The history of Black America also is different from the African and the Caribbean experience. Scholars of these other Black histories are now interpreting those experiences from a point of view quite different from that taken by Afro-American Black scholars.[24]

The primary reason for the differing point of view is the uniquely American slave experience. A second reason is that the African was at home in Africa, the Black homeland. "At-homeness" was a part of the African's argument against colonialization in Africa. A third reason was the peculiar, white use of the Christian message to reinforce slavery as a God-ordained social order. For these reasons, the total Black experience in America, inclusive of the Black

---

[22]See Basil Moore, ed., *The Challenge of Black Theology in South Africa* (Atlanta: John Knox Press, 1974); and Kofi Appiah-Kubi and Sergio Torres, *African Theology en Route* (Maryknoll NY: Orbis Books, 1979).

[23]Wilmore, *Black Religion and Black Radicalism*, 5.

[24]See Noel L. Erskine's *Decolonializing Theology: A Caribbean Perspective* (Maryknoll NY: Orbis Books, 1981) and Appiah-Kubi and Tores, *African Theology en Route.*

Afro-American religious experience, must be understood in terms of its differences from any other history as a unique experience.

In a sense, Black Afro-American history was a planned experience dictated by what C. Eric Lincoln perceptively, if too gently, has called the "host culture." To be Black in America, according to Lincoln, is to be "debarred from certain significant experiences which are available filtered through an alternative set of screens which may determine a different perception and registration of a reality from that common to the larger society."[25] Lincoln argues that the dominant host culture extends its control by codifying its appraisal of minorities, such that these pejorative attitudes become fixed and even formative in the minds of many Black people as well as White. Lincoln comments further on the matter:

> The ramifications of external appraisal of the "host culture" are far-reaching, for among other things, it means that all of the significant institutions which undergird the ontological understanding of a contingent community are either ignored or presupposed as consistent with those of the external evaluator. . . . The conventions of the over-culture have played the dominant role in the architecture of particular Black institutions—as in the case of the Black family.[26]

Both Black people and Black institutions are so undervalued and negatively preconceived by the host culture that Black people themselves—much less Whites—can hardly conceive of Black as equal, even in these better times. The history of unequalness has imposed on Black people what Charles Long calls a "hermeneutical task"—a Black person must learn to understand and conceptualize differently from Whites. Black persons have an added burden of determining who we Black people are on our own terms, not someone else's. Therefore, for a black "to construe the terms *life, liberty,* and *happiness* for non-Europeans" has been a strange task: "My native land has always been for me a strange place."[27]

Because of its peculiar history, the Black community has developed an attitude about itself as "other." According to Long, it is

> a reality so agonizing that it forced us to give up our innocence while at the same time it sustained us in humor, joy, and promise. I am speaking of a quality of the American experience which through its harsh discipline, forever de-

---

[25]C. Eric Lincoln. "The Black Family, the Black Church and the Transformation of Values," *Religion in Life* 47:4 (Winter 1978): 488.

[26]Ibid

[27]Charles Long, "The Black Reality: Toward a Theology of Freedom," *Criterion* (Spring-Summer 1969): 2ff.

stroyed a naive innocence, revealing—a God of creation—a God of our silent tears—a God of our weary years. This may be called "nitty-gritty" pragmatism. It is from this kind of history and involvement with nature, man, and God, that germinates the dense richness out of which profound religious awareness emerged.[28]

This "other" attitude has afforded an inner defense to help Black people persevere in spite of the adverse, negative, and demeaning self-perceptions that have resulted from the treatment they experience simply because they had been born Black. Were it not for this "otherness," Black people as individual ontological entities would be in much deeper trouble with selfhood than they already are. To gloss over the problem of self-identity is to miss the depth dimension of "differentness" of the Black experience. To overlook the problem is to misunderstand the problem of being Black in America and in Long's phrase, to reject the hermeneutical task necessary to acquiring a basic understanding of who a Black person is.

The Black religious experience narrowly defined is unique and therefore drastically different from the religious experience of Whites. Indeed, it is different from any other religious experience. We contend that certain elements have set the Afro-American religious experience apart from all other religious experiences, because the Afro-American religious synthesis retained the best of the African religious heritage and selected from among the best of the slave-masters' religion, White American Christianity. Gayraud S. Wilmore describes the situation this way:

> Christianity alone, as it was usually presented to the slave, adulterated, otherworldly and disengaged from its most radical implications, could not have provided the slave with the religious resources he needed for revolt. It had to be enriched with volatile ingredients of the African religious perspective and, most important of all, with the profound human yearning for freedom that found a channel for expression in the survivals of African religions resident in the early Black churches.[29]

Wilmore acknowledges, of course, that Afro-American Black religion had much in common with ordinary White Protestantism; however, because it was the religion of an oppressed and segregated people, what stands out is its "differentness." Black religion was not a product of drawing rooms in Southern mansions where few Blacks were catechized into traditional Christianity, nor

---

[28]Ibid.

[29]Gayraud S. Wilmore, *Black Religion and Black Radicalism* (New York: Doubleday, 1972) 38.

in the segregated balconies of Northern meeting houses. Rather, says Wilmore, "It was born in Blackness."

> Its most direct antecedents were the quasi-religious quasi-secular meetings which took place on the plantations, unimpeded by White supervision and under the inspired leadership of the first generation of African priests to be taken in slavery. . . . The faith that evolved from the coming together of diverse religious influences was a religion distinctly different from its two major contributors.[30]

The "differentness" that originated in Black religion was perpetuated in what it meant to be born Black in America: Life was constrained within the White-imposed limits of the situational possibilities—what one may not do, where one may not live, what one may not achieve, and what one was ultimately forbidden to experience. This happened simply because one had been debarred from certain types of experiences, thus in the "other" experiences to which C. Eric Lincoln refers.[31]

---

[30]Ibid.

[31]Lincoln, "The Black Family," 488.

CHAPTER TWO

Black Theology
and the God-Concept:
African Roots

The concept of God within the context of African religions traditionally has been misconceived and misinterpreted by most White analysts of the phenomena. The concept of deity was thought to be a highly philosophical idea beyond the grasp of African primitives. In recent years, however, numerous African scholars—John Mbiti, Kofi Appiah-Kubi, Osadolor Imasogie, Allen Aubrey Boesak, Ngindu Mushete and others—have begun to express themselves in terms of "African Theology." Their knowledge of native languages and traditional African religious systems has qualified them to clarify many misunderstandings of African beliefs and correct the pejorative language used for generations to describe African faith—terms such as animism, fetishism, and polytheism.

Somewhat earlier than the current new breed of African Theologian, Father W. Schmidt had pointed out that "a clear acknowledgment and worship of a Supreme Being" existed among the Pigmy people of Central Africa.[1] Besides the "prerogative of unity and Lordship over all other beings," this Supreme Being possesses attributes that parallel those attributed to the Supreme Beings of other religions, religions which are not labeled "primitive." Today without question, anyone familiar with African traditional religions is aware that belief in a Supreme Being, however named, is a common characteristic.

This truth has recently been documented by John S. Mbiti, who studied the religious expressions of over three hundred ethnic groups scattered all over

---

[1]Father W. Schmidt, *The Origin and Growth of Religion*, trans. H. J. Rose (New York: Dial Press, 1931) 191.

the African continent. Mbiti found that with few exceptions the peoples of Africa have a notion of God as a Supreme Being.[2] As the Supreme Being, God is self-sufficient, self-supporting, self-containing, just as he is self-originating. Osadolor Imasogie similarly emphasizes the African understanding of God as Spirit by pointing out that throughout the whole of Africa there are no images or physical representations of God. A knowledgeable reading of current African Theology shows that the "otherness" of God is far from a mere polytheism, with the Supreme Being conceived as just a God among other gods. The Supreme Being was not one who happened to be elevated to the position of a chief of gods. Imasogie rightly reports that, "While Africans accord prominence to the divinities, the divinities are regarded as having been created and appointed to certain ministries by the Supreme Being." In this sense, they might be conceived in the same light as angels within the Jewish and Christian traditions. Imasogie argues for a "bureaucratic monotheism," which he views as preserving "the intrinsic monotheism which undergirds the African religious experience."[3] Africans, one may conclude, did not have to be converted to the worship of the One God when they became Christians. They already worshiped him.

Scholars familiar with African religious traditions acknowledge the existence of what Joseph R. Washington, Jr. calls the "African temperament," which, he contends, has "remarkable resiliency."[4] This resiliency carried over into the Afro-American religious experience and carried African people through the hell of slavery by providing them an unshakable affirmation of life, as Henry H. Mitchell puts it.[5] A resulting corporate mental sturdiness gave the slaves an ability to say "no" to the negations intended to void them of a full and adequate self-affirmation. this is a striking, new view of the Afro-American linkage, because, as Mitchell contends, it is "so nearly identical with the Judaeo-Christian view and because, traditionally, it was automatically assumed that religious views as high as this must have come from Whites,"[6] not from Africans. Afro-American scholars who have come to understand and appre-

---

[2]John S. Mbiti, *African Religions and Philosophy* (London: Heinemann Educational Books, Ltd., 1969) 29.

[3]Osadolor Imasogie, "African Traditional Religion and Christian Faith," *Review and Expositor* 70:3 (Summer 1973): 283ff.

[4]Joseph R. Washington, Jr., *Black Sects and Cults* (Garden City NY: Doubleday, 1972) 97, 84.

[5]Henry H. Mitchell, *Black Belief* (New York: Harper & Row, 1975) 20.

[6]Ibid., 21.

ciate the mind of Africans agree that they tend to be open to new and better ideas, not to replace the old, but to add to what they already have.[7] The "new" of Christianity merely enlarged what was already authentic and foundational to the African God-concept in the mind of Africans who became the slaves of White Christians 300 and more years ago. The linkage between the African's concept of God and the Afro-American's concept of God must be seen against both the long-term religious traditions of African antiquity and the shorter-term religious traditions since slavery. The Africans who were brought to this country after 1619 were not without God; and the fusion of their African religious heritage with newfound Christianity into a single hermeneutical understanding of the God-concept is the unavoidable basis for understanding Afro-American religion. To put it another way, John Mbiti explains that: "In my description [of African beliefs] I have generally used the present tense, as if these ideas are still held and the practices being carried out. He qualifies his explanation as follows:

> It would be wrong to imagine that everything traditional had been changed or forgotten. . . . If anything, the changes are generally on the surface, affecting the material side of life, and only beginning to reach the deeper levels of thinking pattern, language content, mental images, emotions, beliefs and responses in situations of need. Traditional concepts still form the essential background.[8]

We see that African religious thought is permanently en route and developmental, becoming ever new and always renewable, as God becomes a fuller reality.

Indeed, according to Mbiti, Long, and other Black historians of religion, the traditional African God-concept shows a remarkable homogeneity among the African religions, and shares common elements as well with Christianity and ancient Judaism. Concepts of God, nonetheless, are dyed deeply by the historical, geographical, social, and cultural environment of each people; and this accounts for the dissimilarities and occasional lack of oneness. Whether African or Afro-American, however, "broadly speaking, African thought forms are more concrete than abstract."[9] As we mine the African roots of the Afro-American God-concept, we discover in this concreteness of God's attributes an explanation of both the absoluteness and the God-concept in the Afro-American tradition. Mbiti explains:

---

[7]Ibid., 22.

[8]Mbiti, *African Religion*, xi.

[9]Ibid., 39.

Expressed ontologically, God is the origin and the substance of all things. He is "older" than the Zamani period; He is outside and beyond His creation. On the other hand, He is personally involved in His creation, so that it is not outside of Him or His reach. God is thus simultaneously transcendent and immanent; and a balanced understanding of these two extremes is necessary in our discussion of African conceptions of God.[10]

Mbiti elsewhere observes that "African knowledge of God is expressed in proverbs, short statements, songs, prayers, names, myths, stories and religious ceremonies." These are passed down from one generation to another as a part of the oral religious tradition. When these traditions eventually are written down, Mbiti instructs, "one should not, therefore, expect long dissertations about God."[11] Nevertheless, merely because the oral traditions of the Africans are different from the writing habits of other cultures does not mean that God is a stranger to African peoples. "In traditional life there are no atheists," says Mbiti; "this is summarized in an old Ashanti proverb that 'no one shows a child the Supreme Being.' "[12] This means that "everybody knows of God's existence almost by instinct, and even children know Him."[13]

THE AFRO-AMERICAN GOD-CONCEPT AND SOME PROBLEMS ON THE BLACK THEOLOGICAL AGENDA

The Problem of the Abstract

If the existence of God is the most important fact, then one's concept of God determines what he or she believes about everything else. However, if one is to understand the full implications of the God-concept in the history of Black religious experience, one must discern that when Black theologians speak of God, they mean more than a reference to an abstract ontological assumption.

The concept of God conceived solely as an abstract term conveys an implied meaning that is so strong and powerful, one can encounter it and be grasped by it, and yet miss a full and adequate knowledge of what the God-concept can mean to the person of faith. If one does not acquire this knowledge of God adequately, a merely acquired belief in God may leave one unawakened to the ethical demands God makes on one's life. A solely abstract

---

[10]John S. Mbiti, *Concepts of God in Africa* (New York: Praeger, 1969).

[11]Mbiti, *African Religions,* 37.

[12]Ibid., 38.

[13]Ibid., 18ff.

concept of God cannot carry the weight of authentic faith, since such a faith implies that a person ought to move beyond belief alone to responsible action under God. Belief in God as a mere abstract concept has caused the current, widespread crisis of faith. Theologian Karl Rahner defines the abstract concept of God, as the word beyond words, the word that points to more than words.

> The real word "God" is not simply identical with the word "God" which appears in a dictionary lost among thousands of other words. For this dictionary word "God" only represents the real word which becomes present for us from out of the wordless texture of all words through their context and through their unity and totality, which itself exists and is present for us. This real word confronts us with ourselves and with reality as a whole, at least as a question. . . . Its demise can be thought of only along with the death of man himself.[14]

If Black Theology is to serve the Black church, it must make the God-concept more than a mere abstraction. It must seek a living and usable God, who can be known among his people.

Black Human Aspirations and the God-Concept

Unlike certain Western traditions in philosophy, psychology, and even theology, Afro-American religious thought has never claimed that religion is solely an expression of the human desire to replace God. In Afro-American thought, God's power is not conceived as counter to human personhood or human power. In contrast to Western psychological and theological ideas that set God apart as the Totally Other, Black Theology has concerned itself less with the question "Does God exist, and how?" than with the question: "Does God care?" God-talk within the Black religious tradition has spoken of God as coextensive. The nature of God in the Black religious experience is both to "be" and to "let be." In this sense, God and human development are viewed not as separate and counter, but rather as complementary to each other. J. Deotis Roberts is right when he asserts that "so closely are God and man tied together in theological reflections that it is almost a matter of indifference whether one begins reflection upon man and moves to God or whether one begins with God and moves to man. In the end, God and men must be considered together in any worthy theological understanding of the Christian faith."[15]

---

[14]Karl Rahner, *Foundations of Christian Faith* (New York: Seabury Press, 1978) 50-51.

[15]J. Deotis Roberts, *Liberation and Reconciliation: A Black Theology* (Philadelphia: Westminster Press, 1973) 76.

Both in African and Afro-American thought, God, as an "outstanding reality," has a central place, because he is equated with human existence itself. For Black people, aspiring to God is the same as aspiring to one's future, for the future is grounded in God's being. Traditionally, this has never meant replacing God's qualities with one's own being. Rather, it has meant that by the help of God, one creates one's own being. Reading African and Afro-American literature, and even literature from the most adverse times of slavery, one must conclude that Black people have never viewed their growth or development as a conscious competition with God. Blacks, never viewing themselves as being more than human, have always conceived of themselves as aspiring to be God-like by doing God's will. Religious life means at least becoming one's own best possible self under God. Religion as self-affirmation on these terms can never be counter to God nor ever consider God a threat or barrier to human fulfillment and development. Human development has a meaning for Black people that is different from most Whites. Neither threat nor rival, God is, rather, the very basis or ground of the creature's fullest possible self-realization. That is what Black religious experience is all about: It is about being and becoming more human under God.

God and the Ultimate Human Quest

Any meaningful concept of religion must deal with the ultimacy of God, his relation to his creation, and how human beings exist within God's creation. The religious quest defined by current Black Theology presupposes that God is not found within humankind but confronts us externally in a divine-human encounter wherein the creature is addressed by the Creator. In this sense, human beings become aware of themselves as being akin to God because he addresses them as persons in relation to himself. In such a two-sided encounter, God manifests himself as Supreme Person and human beings understand themselves on the basis of how they conceive of themselves under God. On this premise the quality of the Black religious quest rests. Abstractions about God may differ among thinkers but the Black religious quest must relate to the question of what God ultimately means for Black people.

At the same time, the Black religious quest is always a turning from all human and earthly concerns toward the Ultimate. Should the Black religious experience lose the relation to God, it becomes devoid of the needed quality of authentic eschatology. Black eschatology is the theological knot that ties God and humanity, being and becoming, together.

The Black religious quest is authentic only if it is conceived under a God who discloses himself to human beings as a Supreme Personal Being. It follows that such a God does not ever demand the sacrifice of finite beings, individually or collectively. God, rather, as Supreme Personal Being fulfills the ultimate human quest that has its final realization in a trans-historical consummation. Cosmic reality as God's creation has become a reality only under God and in relation to God; therefore, cosmic reality continues to be the arena of God's action and, the arena also of human actions under God in response to him personally. This must mean that "God" is the a name for the "Thou-Quality" of the world.

Although God is in the world, he should not be conceived as being merely in the world, nor "at one" with the world. God's full reality can be known or realized within the world only partly. For this reason, the Black religious quest on the one hand is directed toward a God who is central to all human aspirations, who is the concreteness of the religious quest, because it is God and God alone who must address human beings, if they are ever to become fully aware of themselves. To be and do this, God must be conceived as one who permeates every part of human existence, every human concern. On the other hand, God transcends the world and all human existence; and is conceived ontologically by Black religious experience as a personal being whose entity is more than the total of either the natural order or human existence. God is both historical and trans-historical, immanent in the world, and, yet, not at one with the world.

The human act of the Black religious quest is a turning to God, by which act of turning, human beings become aware of themselves at the highest possible level of self-awareness. This is so simply because in such an encounter, God has addressed them. Black people cannot talk about liberation, freedom, and salvation within history unless they include the God of their eschatological future, to whom they turn in order to become whatever they shall be. Black theologians cannot talk about God all the while alleging that their God-talk is unrelated to the needs of Black people in this world. This means that Black Theology must reaffirm the God of the Black religious experience as the One in whom the final destiny of Black people and the future of all reality are represented as one. Ultimate liberation, freedom, and salvation can be derived from God alone. Thus, it follows that liberation, freedom and salvation are God's promise of the future; and God is the reality of the future that cannot be separated from the religious quest. Saving faith must see God, first, as a now and a future promise, and finally, as an ultimate fulfillment. God is related to a future both as the "now" and the "not yet" that cannot be derived apart from God. In the Black religious experience, the seeker must perceive God as being future as well as present. It must be so, if God is to be the God of the Black person's ultimate quest. In this sense, God is at one with the struggle of the oppressed

The Problem of Divine Unreality

The task of reconceiving God's reality has visited the Black religious community by a different route than it took to the White counterpart. Nevertheless, that problem has come. The shape of this visitation concerns what God is doing in the world today, and how God is involved in the liberation, freedom, and ultimate salvation of Black people. For this reason, I argue in the preceding paragraphs that Black Theology does not merely assume the existence of God without insisting upon a discussion of God's ontological personhood and what God's Supreme Personal Being means for human existence. The reality of God bears directly on questions of the earthly struggle for liberation and freedom. An understanding of divine reality as related to earthly struggle is central to the task of Black Theology.

Expressions of unbelief have lately found their way into Black religious experience. These expressions of unbelief are indirectly related to four main characteristics of the Civil Rights Movement and to what Vincent Harding has called "the religion of Black power."[16]

First, questions about whether God cares stem from the failure in the first phases of the Civil Rights Movement to achieve clear and complete victories for Black people. This situation caused a breakdown in the simple conception of God as an absolute Being who meets all needs and solves all problems. For less religious Black people, God seemed to have withheld help directly from those who had believed in and depended on God to help solve the problem of racism in the world and even in the church.

Second, the question of whether or not God cares about human pain has been raised against the impossibility Black people experienced when they attempted to reconcile their suffering with the absolute power and goodness of God. William R. Jones was the first contemporary Black theologian to speak directly to the problem of Black suffering when faced with the religious assertion: "God cares!" By asking the question, "Is God a White racist?" Jones made the problem of evil a more specialized concern of Black Theology. Jones requires theology, especially Black Theology, to provide with integrity a miracle-working God who will set Black people free all at once, in one "mighty act" such as the Exodus of the Israelites from Egypt. He posed the question of theodicy for Black Theology in this way: "How can blacks know that God disapproves of black suffering except by his *elimination of it, except by bringing it to an immediate halt?* . . . The scandal of the particularity of black suffering

---

[16]Vincent Harding, "The Religion of Black Power," in *The Religious Situation, 1968,* ed. Donald R. Cutler (Boston: Beacon Press, 1968) 3-38.

can be answered only by an appeal to the particularity of God's liberating activity—an Exodus-type event for blacks."[17]

Although William R. Jones was asking more of God than is revealed to Black Theology, he was not asking more than has been a barrier to Black belief and adherence to God.

Third, the radical Black Power mentality and the few successes of the Civil Rights Movement have both heightened Black people's sense of their own ability and lessened the urgency of the question as to whether God cares. At least fragmented victories have been realized through Black people's own independent actions. Time has made apparent that radical actions, dress, and thought may offer the only hopeful options for Black people in contemporary America. Black Theology must determine whether change can best be achieved by more action, or if signs now point to more radical actions, more direct in purpose, if less symbolic in content.

Fourth, a new sense of freedom that somewhat excludes religion is now growing in the Black community. This situation is new to the Black experience. No longer are civil rights victories necessarily attributed to God. The time may come when the Black religious mood becomes nostalgia for a religious past, but without a fully conceptualized God-concept. Many Black people these days, even while they still accept, or at least, do not deny the mysterious, the holy, or even the transcendent in human life, have a nonreligious mood. Their God-concept has little or no concrete meaning. God's reality has been played down to the point that many feel no need for a living God's role in human affairs. However, some Black militants of late have gone to extremes to seek, to find, and to celebrate new expressions of religion amid the many new demands and new choices of ordinary life. These are attempts to find religious meaning short of a conceptual faith in God.

If Vincent Harding was right, godless religion is now, to some degree, a current reality in "an explosive Black world where Gods are dying and being resurrected at every turn." He observed "the first stages of public doubt and questioning of God by Black folk" and concluded that "significant elements of the Black community have joined the rest of the society in its movements towards a practical agnosticism." He further remarked on "the arrival of new Gods; the Allah of the Nation of Islam, the new-old Gods of Yoruba and the Housa peoples, the nameless, still anticipated Gods of profoundly searching young revolutionaries."[18]

---

[17]William R. Jones, *Is God a White Racist?* (Garden City NY: Doubleday, 1973) 115-17.

[18]Vincent Harding, preface to the Atheneum edition of Benjamin E. Mays's *The Negro's God* (New York: Atheneum Press, 1973) i.

These ideas, now less than two decades old, are losing their validity. One wonders if Dr. Harding would express these same views now that Elijah Muhammad, the elder statesman of the Nation of Islam, and the radical Malcolm X have been succeeded by a domesticated religious denomination of the middle-class business-minded; now that Eldridge Cleaver has become a "born-again Christian," and now that the Black Panthers have been attempting to have church. The truth remains that a deeper need than ever for a reconception of the reality of God perdures. The signs point to a process of reconceptualization that has already begun. This does not mean that Black people are where they ought to be in the process! Indeed, the need is always current to work at the process of reconceiving the reality of God—a churchman or theologian is not realistic who would conclude otherwise. This is the reason for engaging the Black theological community in much needed theological God-talk.

The Problem of the Silence of God

The divine unreality becomes the reality of God when a community of faith responds to the reality of divine unreality. Because God is not direct in his approach to human beings—because God is silent and hides himself—God is sometimes presumed to be nonexistent. Absolute proof of God's existence is beyond the scope of mere human reason. That is why Black Theology is written for a church who simply assume God to be. This does not mean, of course, that a quest for the true knowledge of God's existence is unnecessary; but "knowledge of God's existence" is possible without "having faith in God." Black Theology knows that what God does for us in faith is greater than what God does for us in knowledge.

Many American Black people, first in slavery and later in other kinds of suffering, have asked: "If God exists, why does he choose to remain hidden and silent?" Theologian John Hick has argued the case most cogently that a successful absolute proof of God's existence would negate the human freedom of free acceptance of God. God is silent, Hick argues, because an absolute proof of his existence would negate faith; God does not want to compel his creatures to belief or coerce them into faith. God's silence is God's respect for his creatures' freedom, and his hiddenness is the space our ability to choose needs in order to believe freely on its own. [19]

The Black experience in American history has predetermined that Black Theology must concern itself in every way with freedom of every kind. Therefore, Black Theology affirms what the Christian faith teaches, that true religion is possible only when a free decision is made in faith's free response to

---

[19]John Hick, *Evil and the God of Love* (London: Macmillan, 1966).

God's love. If our knowledge of God were absolute, our choices would be limited and faith would not be free. An objective justification of faith, moreover, would have the same effect: Faith must be subjective, because if an objective proof of faith were possible at all, all free decisions made in faith-knowledge would be eliminated. Human beings would no longer be free to say "yes" or "no" to God, just as we do not say "yes" or "no" to gravity. If God could be proved, like a law of nature or a mathematical formula, but in the personal sphere, then faith in God would become a law and a formula and God would become a demanding master over his faith-slaves.

Hick further contends that God presents himself to his creatures in silent, hidden, indirect, and uncertain ways—instead of displaying himself unambiguously—so that room for doubt will be left open. God does this, as Hick teaches and Black Theology knows, so that we dependent human beings can come to know God as the One who makes the total difference for us; and, in so doing, come by way of faith to full consciousness of God's existence and, thereby, to set ourselves in faith freely under the absolute divine claim.[20]

God is the way he is, and it appears that he has deliberately created an ambiguous world for us to live in so that we shall not be compelled to be conscious of him. But, out here on the periphery of all creation, we recognize our human self as a created and totally dependent being, longing for its highest good in relationship to the dark, unspeaking God who resides at the absolute divine center of all reality. Black Theology thus accepts that one who becomes conscious of God in this indirect way remains a free and responsible being forever, remains faithful in the knowledge that he or she will never know God in the absolute fullness of God's divine personal being. The faith-knowledge of Black Theology abides content in the assumption that God exists, willing to go on living in the presence of that highest personal being whose very existence is merely assumed. Faith is "at one" with the never-ending search for God, and the search is "at one" with Black faith. The very searching itself is what sets us under the absolute claim of God; and this is, as it should be, the central tenet of Black Theology: To know God is never conceptually to possess God in the fullness of God's being, but is to let God be free and, thereby, to remain free ourselves to quest or not, to search or not, to believe or not in the absolutely personal, divine, and holy loving God.

God and the Search for Black Personhood

With the modern emphasis on empirical concerns about practical problems, a solely abstract concept of God will not suffice. Theology must find a

---

[20]Ibid.

new perspective for interpreting God as usable, intelligible, and pragmatic. Only Black Theology has the indigenous experience to frame such a God-concept for the Black religious community of faith. This empirical God-concept for Blacks will have to do with leadership, education, survival, and justice.

Not since the origin of the Black church has the faith of the Black community been so much in need of spiritual and intellectual leadership from the Black church. Traditionally, Black people have found the source of their true identity in the Black church—the one place where a Black person could be an authentic leader. The Black church, even now, is that one place where Black individuals can become somebody at a time when beyond the church's confines, they are still mere nobodies.

Benjamin E. Mays revealed the central role that God played in the human development of Black people when he wrote of his desire for education during youth: "My prayers were all variations of the same theme: a petition to God to enable me to get away to school. My desire for an education was not only a dream, but a goal that drove me and prodded me day and night."[21]

Mays also reflects on the role that God played in the lives of Black slaves, when they perceived God as the only one to guarantee their survival.[22] Almost from their first encounter with the Christian God-concept, the slaves pictured God as an instrument of survival and an agent related to their struggle for freedom. They already believed in an ancient God of love, who created and cared for his children, even suffering slaves. But they had an absolute faith that this God was also a God of justice and vengeance, who hated evil and was against oppression. They were convinced that their God would one day destroy oppression, slavery, and all the evildoers. Only this faith in the ultimate righteousness of God enabled the slaves to bridge the contradiction between their situation and what they thought the situation ought to be. Faith in the God of a radically different future enabled them to go on living.

The slaves could not have withstood slavery without the abiding strength of their updated, Afro-American God-concept. To maintain personal dignity, moral integrity, and self-respect under the crushing effects of cruelties imposed on them by Whites, the slaves found strength and a sustaining power in their adaptations of a newly conceptualized God.[23] For the slave, the God of the Afro-American religious experience was a new creation. God was an updated, previously African God, seen anew according to a new and unique God-concept.

---

[21]Benjamin E. Mays, *Born to Rebel* (New York: Charles Scribner's Sons, 1971) 36.

[22]Ibid.

[23]Harry V. Richardson, *Dark Salvation* (Garden City NY: Doubleday, 1976) 28-29.

CHAPTER THREE

Toward an Afro-Americanized God-Concept

THE HERMENEUTICAL PROBLEM OF A NEW GOD'S REALITY

For the Afro-American community of faith, the concept of God has always been a deep hermeneutical problem, requiring ever new interpretations and broader understandings. This hermeneutical task causes the knowledgeable Black theologian to look beneath the surface of words to find the truth of their meaning in conceptual understanding. To be able to comprehend the Afro-American God-concept, indeed, demands development of a new frame of reference for interpreting God by way of the Afro-American religious experience.

A number of points of view are clearly not the correct starting point for developing an Afro-American hermeneutic. Were one to begin with Karl Barth's understanding of revelation, for example, the Afro-American concept of God would be totally unacceptable as a revelatory expression of the Black Christian's faith. Barth wrote, "Revelation does not link up with a human religion which is already present and practiced. It contradicts it, just as religion previously contradicted revelation. It displaces it, just as religion previously displaced revelation."[1]

This view negates any new revelation. For Barth, without Christ there can be no religion, and even with Christ, revelation is not religion. According to

---

[1] Karl Barth, *Church Dogmatics,* vol. 2, eds. G. W. Bromily and T. F. Torrance (Edinburgh, Scotland: T. & T. Clark, 1956) 303.

Barth's view, the African religion of the slave ought not to have acquired a new dimension from its encounter with the Christian religion of the slave masters during the pre-Civil-War period. Total negation of the African religious heritage would have had to occur, if Barth's view were completely valid. Black people's conversion to Christianity would have had to have been, for them, a completely new religion based only upon the religion of the slave master. This is how most Whites thought of the Christian faith. But, of course, Barth's notion argues against history, which is always a dangerous thing to do.

Another inadequate starting point is Cecil Cone's view. He accepts too fully that the survival of African religion was the central motif in the African's conversion to Christianity. Cone argues that Africans "were not converted to Christianity, but they converted Christianity to themselves." Drawing on his extensive study of Black religious experiences, Cone's premise becomes an absolute assumption and suggests reductionism, such that Cecil Cone goes beyond his own basic contention. He correctly says that God is "the Almighty Sovereign God," which he incorrectly deduces to be an African conception of God.[2]

To conceptualize God differently from another model is not to reduce God to one's own idea of what God should be. The slaves brought with them from Africa an African understanding of God, but when they were converted they reconceptualized God, thus acquiring a new—and, Christians would say—a deeper and clearer revelation of what God means for Black human existence. The truth of God's almighty sovereign Being was authenticated to the African slaves in the experiences of Black suffering. The reconceptualization of God grew and flourished in Black religious temperament to produce a viable, indigenous religious orientation to God conceived as concerned with Black freedom and Black human integrity.

Yet a third beginning point from which we do not want to start is John Mbiti's. He writes in the post-colonial context of late twentieth-century Africa and believes that Africans have tended to reject all aspects of the Christian faith that did not penetrate those areas of life which they felt required salvation. "Thus, it is the experience of faith in God of might and power which mediates acts of redemption and salvation from those forces which work against the physical integrity of the individual and the community."[3]

The experience of Afro-American Blacks, however, was different; and the Afro-American Black theological agenda is different from, although related

---

[2]Cecil Wayne Cone, *The Identity Crisis in Black Theology* (Nashville: The African Methodist Episcopal Church Press, 1975) 32.

[3]John Mbiti, "Our Savior as an African Experience," in *Christian and the Spirit,* eds. Smalley and Linders (Cambridge MA: Cambridge University Press, 1973) 400ff.

to, the neo-colonial Black religious agenda. Africa was and is the African's home; therefore, land is a part of the African's indigenous religious experience. To have one's homeland colonialized is to be dispossessed. The African struggle to free the people and the land from colonial masters was different from the antislavery struggle of the landless, homeless Afro-American. The resulting God-consciousness is also different. Common to both experiences, to be sure, is the belief that God rescues people when all other help is ineffective or has seemingly been exhausted. Redemptive rescue from slavery had to include freedom from the material and physical dangers destroying Black people since their first encounter with the evil in its several particular expressions. God, in both the African religious tradition and in the Afro-American Christian tradition, was conceived as a caring God, able to do all things; because God, to be adequate, must be absolute in power and might. But in the African expectation, God and the land were bound up together in ways impossible for Black Afro-Americans who had been permanently uprooted and made into a nation of enslaved pilgrims.

Nor, finally, do we want to set the stage for an Afro-Americanized concept of God by suggesting that this search is new or unique to Afro-Americans. Reconceiving God authentically for and by Blacks caused the Afro-American God to enter a set of unique human experiences in a unique historical situation. Nonetheless, Blacks share similarities with all other peoples who, in times of struggle and national or ethnic crisis, have turned to God in their search for solid ground. The search for a new God-concept has taken place in this century, as Vincent Harding reminded us, "no less significantly in Ireland, Germany, than in Kenya and the Congo."[4] The Black people's search for an adequate God-concept is new only in its particularity and in its reconceptualized God-content.

THE PARTICULARITY OF THE BLACK GOD-CONCEPT

In studying the Afro-American Black people's search for a usable concept of God, a number of beginning points must be kept in mind, if the the assessment is to be representative and authentic.

First, any concept of God that excludes personal relevancy is inadequate and incomplete. Human beings need God in order to live at the highest level of self-confidence, self-certainty, and self-respect. This is why theology always has to be brought back to the basic human self as a criterion for a full understanding of God.

---

[4]Vincent Harding, "The Religion of Black Power," *The Religious Situation* (1968): 31.

Jürgen Moltmann reminds us that the certainty of God presupposes the certainty of self. From an Afro-American point of view, unless one can in some highly personal way relate God to self and self to God, then God and the person have not acquired an adequate relationship that is basic to and necessary for a true faith-experience relationship. God is still an alien to the person who has not come to a full self-knowledge of being a person under God. In the long history of the God-human relationship probably no other theologian was clearer on this than was Augustine. He insisted that knowledge of the self is no longer a part of the mere knowledge of the world, but is related more certainly to a knowledge of God. Moltmann was thinking about Augustine's view when he wrote: "The world is God's work, but man is God's image. That means that every human being finds in himself the mirror in which he can perceive God. The knowledge of God in his image is surer than the knowledge of God from his works. So the foundation of true self-knowledge is to be found in God."[5] Accepting Augustine's and Moltmann's concurring statements, we gain insight as to why we humans feel an urgent need to make God known to all people in the light of who we are. Especially is this true when we have been subjected to alien views both of our "self" and our "God."

Second, one must be aware that God comes to each person in the existential context of the individual's personal being. God addresses each person as he or she is, and God is conceived and understood in the reciprocal light of who that person is at that moment. Subjectively and objectively, God's self-address to every person is both social and personal. When God makes himself known to a person, something happens to God in his self-disclosure, as well as to the human being to whom God is revealed. In this sense, the physical-spiritual nature of revelation is consistent with the physical-spiritual nature of personhood. God addresses the true nature of an individual's being. How better, then, can God be understood than in the light of who we are?

If we are Black, must not God's self-address to us be related to the blackness of the persons being addressed? God's address to Black people includes his knowledge of Black awareness, Black pride, Black self-respect, and the deep desire for full, Black self-determination. God's self-address to Black people includes their political desire to be free and aspiration to be equal in every way. If God needs to become Black in his self-address to Black persons, then God becomes Black. In this sense, God's self-address to the Black person takes on a particular form and conveys a particular message. It is personal, and yet it is to a whole people.

---

[5]Jürgen Moltmann, *The Trinity and the Kingdom: The Doctrine of of God* (New York: Harper and Row Publishers, 1981) 14.

In this true sense, God addresses a man in his maleness and a woman in her femaleness; God becomes "at one" with her or him. God has a personal word in relation to who he or she is at the level of their gender. Because God "will be whoever he will be" and because God is "everything in everyone," we need not belabor the question as to whether God is male or female. God relates to the person and to the people in the light of who he or she is and in the light of who a people might be. God's absolute being becomes relevant to the individual or the people addressed, color included.

Third, the attempt to study the development of this search must include awareness of why the search is necessary. Being Black in White America has always posed for Black people the hermeneutical task of understanding themselves. To add God to the task is merely to compound the confusion. Yet the task is a necessary one; for it is foundational to one's faith and one's identity. Black people in a white land, slave people in a free land, rejected people in a bountiful land, one might well conclude that it is impossible to understand one's self as an Afro-American at all—as impossible as attempting to reconcile being and nonbeing, as impossible, indeed, as reconciling the agony of the whole Black experience itself.

W. E. B. Du Bois spoke of this agony when he wrote:

> It is a peculiar sensation, this double-consciousness, this sense of always looking at one's self through the eyes of others, of measuring one's soul by that type of world that looks on in amused contempt and pity. One ever feels his two-ness—an American, a Negro; two souls, two thoughts, two unreconciled strivings; two warring ideals in one dark body, whose dogged strength alone keep it from being torn asunder.[6]

Only a deep relationship to a personal God, who addressed Black people in terms of who they were, kept Black people self-assured and with a sense of their true humanity.

In the fourth place, one must know that Afro-Americans did not embrace the Christian religion without questions, rational adaptations, reinterpretations, and appropriations. They rejected those parts of the Christianity of their White masters that did not fit into what they needed for a "redemptive" application.

Representative of the questions which the conditions of the slave period placed upon the minds and lips of the slave are the following from the prayer of Nathaniel Paul. "Why slavery?" he asked.

Tell me, ye mighty waters, why did ye sustain the ponderous load of misery?

---

[6]James Farmer, "White Liberals and Black Liberation," in *Is Anybody Listening to Black America?*, ed. C. Eric Lincoln (New York: Seabury Press, 1968) 38.

Or speak, ye winds, and say why it was that you executed your office to waft them onward to the still more dismal state; and ye proud waves, why did you refuse to lend your aid and to have overwhelmed them with your billows? Then should they have slept sweetly in the bosom of the great deep, and so have been hid from sorrow. And, oh thou immaculate God, be not angry with us, while we come into this thy sanctuary and make bold inquiry in thy holy temple, why it was that thou didst look on with the calm of indifference of an unconcerned spectator, when thy holy law was violated, thy divine authority despised and a portion of thine own creatures reduced to a state of mere vassalage and misery.[7]

To muse thus, to agonize thus, and then to find an answer within his own strength to reason, represents the genius of the Black person of faith. Indeed, such must have been the thoughts of the Black members of the audience who heard the Reverend Paul on the fifth day of July, 1827, at an Abolition Rally in New York State. Nathaniel Paul found an answer to his own question when he further mused:

Hark, while He answers from on high; hear Him proclaiming from the skies. "Be still, and know that I am God! Clouds and darkness are around about me; yet, righteousness and judgment are the habitation of my throne. I do my will and pleasure in the heavens above, and in the earth beneath; it is my sovereign prerogative to bring good out of evil and cause the wrath of man to praise me, and the remainder of that wrath I will restrain."[8]

For the Black Afro-American of faith, there have never been easy answers. "How long, Lord?" may well have been the most frequently asked question of the period. Bishop Daniel Payne, Bishop of the A.M.E. Churchs described the collective quest when he said: "With God, one day is a thousand years and a thousand years is as one day. 'Trust in Him and he will bring slavery and all of the outrages to an end.' These words from the spirit world acted on my troubled soul like water on a burning fire and my aching heart was soothed and relieved from its burden of woes."[9]

Like Job of the Bible, the faith of the slaves and their Afro-American children was never a faith without questions. But, then, for Black people, God

---

[7]Nathaniel Paul, "An Address on the Celebration of the Abolition of Slavery in New York," delivered July 5, 1827, Library of Congress, 15-16.

[8]Ibid.

[9]Daniel A. Payne, *A Recollection of Slavery* (Nashville: The African Methodist Episcopal Church Publishing House, 1888) 27.

has never been one who seemed to desire only easy answers, either for himself or for human beings. This is a central dimension of the Black religious experience. This is why, even in our time of relative ease and comfort, a Black professor at Yale could ask, "Is God a White racist?" At the same time, belief within the Black religious experience has also sustained Black people by a faith that God's acceptance of human suffering and evil has never been passive. Although God seems to allow evil and suffering to exist in the world, it is also clear that God always opposes evil; and we miss the reality of his working if we do not discern that God's opposition to evil is often misunderstood. He does not employ all available means to have his way or to coerce his free humans; he may even suffer a seeming defeat. A mature reading of history suggests that, although finite human beings are right in feeling that the world could be improved, God himself seems to be in no great hurry to transform his creation's basic structures into perfection. God, it seems, favors a democratic rule for existence, with an ultimate movement toward some ideal known only to God, at which time God's absolute rule will prevail and God's ultimate good shall be established. Meanwhile, the person of faith must recognize that the world is characterized by a mixture of finite victories and defeats that produce perpetually ambiguous combinations of both good and evil. Even in the days of deepest human suffering, when evil seemed to prevail, the faith of the Black religious experience has believed in the ultimate victory of good over evil. Indeed, one cannot read the history of the slaves' experiences, the dreams of freedom, the aspirations expressed in story, tales, and song without realizing that they contain ambiguous combinations in recognition both of good and evil. In all the records of the Black religious experience, the feeling is evident that the slaves, like all other human beings, sensed they had a personal role to play in their struggle for liberation. Both the secular and the sacred literatures of the time give evidence of this feeling. This feeling is the fifth beginning point of the Afro-American God-concept.

Henry J. Young interprets the literature of the period, 1755-1940, to say that voices such as Nathaniel Paul, Richard Allen, David Walker, Nat Turner, Daniel A. Payne, James W. C. Pennington, and Henry Highland Garnett were at one in expressing the Black person's feeling that he had a role to play in the struggle for liberation and freedom.[10] In 1844, Garnett expressed the view then current: "The humblest peasant is as free in the sight of God as the proudest monarch that ever swayed a scepter. Liberty is a spirit sent out from God and, like its great author, is no respector of persons. Brethren, the time

---

[10]Henry J. Young, *Major Black Religious Leaders, 1755-1940* (New York: Abingdon Press, 1977).

has come when you must act for yourselves. It is an old and true saying that, 'if hereditary bondsmen would be free, they must, themselves, strike the blow.' "[11]

For the Afro-American, hope has always been a kind of restlessness filled with protest. It seemed patient only on the surface; but it was ever a deep troubling beneath the calm that would not be stilled. Faith must not only be a consolation in suffering and times of evil but also a protest of divine promise against suffering and evil. For one to be sustained by hope in times of great stress, that person must be assured that God is fighting not only with the individual but also against evil and suffering, that God is able to help one overcome all odds.

Making use of Cecil Cone's contention that "Africans converted Christianity to themselves," it might be more accurate to say that a process of acceptance and rejection took place. Blacks rejected those aspects of Christianity that did not fit their need for survival and redemption, and they accepted the parts in keeping with their aspirations to be free. Within this process, the God of Christianity was reconceptualized, as he was measured against the struggle for liberation and equated with the intention and will of an Afro-Americanized people of faith.

The sole reason Black people have not rebelled against a God who has seemed, at times, indifferent to their conditions of servitude and despair, was that they did not conceive of God in the way that their masters of the host culture did. Charles Long wrote: "God is different down where prayer is hardly more than a moan, down there close to where life and death seem almost equitable."[12] In times of stress, God is a different kind of God. There, where the believer encounters the true and almighty sovereign God, and only then can one know God at the ultimate edge of finite existence. The power of God so perceived is always a God reconceptualized and reinterpreted in the light of an ever-new and more mature understanding. Black people's God is different, because Black people have met their God under a unique set of human conditions. How often in the wretchedness of existence have Black people known God as the only one who was with them! Not their masters, certainly, and, often, not even themselves, but only God, who had constituted their humanity, accorded them a sense of self-worth and "somebodyness." They were children of God; their soul was free.

---

[11]Quoted in Benjamin E. Mays, *The Negro's God* (New York: Atheneum, 1968) 46.

[12]Charles H. Long, "Black Religion: Re-orientation in Perspective," unpublished paper, delivered at the Consultation in Atlanta, April 1970.

This conversion of God was a radical and necessary theological move for the slaves and their Afro-American descendants: The Afro-Americanized God became the bedrock of Black identity and sanity. Charles Long says that the God-encounter provided Black people a norm for self-criticism not derived from their oppressors—the chief sin was seen as the opposite of faith; doubt became the sin of sins in many Black communities of faith.[13] This element of faith is unavoidable to anyone familiar with the civil rights struggles of the sixties and early seventies. Divine freedom—the very meaning of faith—is an Afro-Americanized God's presence in Black people's existence whereby they are given a new life that resides in a concept of God constantly being renewed. Even in the midst of bondage and defeat, Black people have always been able to celebrate, not bondage or defeat, but, rather, human existence in spite of dehumanizing external bondage and the infernal exile of civil rights' defeats. Cecil Cone concludes that "the divine and the divine alone occupies the position of ultimacy in Black religion." Indeed, an encounter with the divine is what constitutes the essential core of Black religion. That encounter—of a Black person with God, who is Black—is the Black religious experience.[14]

TOWARD THE IMAGE OF A GOD WHO IS BLACK

An understanding of God's color has been at the center of the ancient tradition of the Black religious experience. But in this new day, some Blacks are writing history of a newfound earthly existence under and in relation to a newly conceived God. Much in the Black religious experience has changed; and God's Being is seen differently in the light of these unusual conditions. But one thing about God does not change for Black people—his color. Describing Africanized Christianity, Cecil Cone cites Henry McNeal Turner.

> Every race of people since time began, who have attempted to describe their God by words, or by paintings, or carvings, or by any other form or figure, have conveyed the idea that the God who made them and shaped their destiny was symbolized in themselves, and why should not the Negro believe that he resembles God as much as any other people? We do not believe that there is any hope for a race of people who do not believe that they look like God.[15]

---

[13]Ibid.

[14]Cone, *The Identity Crisis*, 143-144.

[15]Henry McNeal Turner, *Respect Black: The Writings and Speeches of Henry McNeal Turner*, ed. Edwin S. Redkey (New York: The Arno Press 1971) 176. See also *Voice of Missions*, 5 April 1898, and *Christian Recorder*, 16 May 1898.

Throughout religious history, human beings have invariably conceptualized God according to their existential situation and in terms of their self-understanding, the ontological concept of God being influenced by historical, psychosocial, and cultural factors. God may well have ontological being over and above and quite apart from how humans project the divine nature, character, and personhood; nevertheless, God as personal being is always conceived or conceptualized, to a great degree, in anthropomorphic terms derived from the ways human beings view themselves. Theologians of every stripe who have agreed that God has personhood have also agreed that a full and complete understanding of God is beyond all human comprehension. All mere human attempts to speak of God are related to one's own humanness. This, to repeat, is because we see God through human eyes, subjecting the God-concept to the limits of our own humaness. Here, because I want to talk about God's color only in relation to Black people, I discuss God's blackness and his moral character. If one were White, God would look White.

In reading the history of African religions prior to the influence of Western missionary, White Christianity, one finds little mention of the color of God in Black or White terms. In African language and culture, "blackness" has no negative connotations. John S. Mbiti observed that: "African concepts of God are strongly colored," meaning that concepts of God are influenced by the "historical, geographical, social, and cultural background or environment of each people."[16] Only after Black people had been exposed to the arrogance of the Western White mentality did the color of God become more than an easy "anthropomorphic assumption." The color of God may have been an easy assumption for pre-missionary Africans; however, in the context of pro-White colonial culture, where one was treated less than human because of color, it became psychologically impossible for Black people not to have problems with God's color.

The color of God is a recurring theme throughout all Black religious thought. David J. Bosch, in a discussion of when to pinpoint the beginning of Black Theology in America and Africa, alluded to the first known occasion in the Western hemisphere of a perception of Christian deity as black.

> About the year 1700 a Congolese girl, Kimpa Vita, with the baptismal name of Beatrice, began appearing in public as a prophetess. She claimed to have had several visions and to have experienced death and resurrection. She said that Saint Anthony had taken possession of her and had commanded her to preach and to teach. She, like Saint Francis of Assisi, first gave away all of her possessions. . . .

---

[16]Mbiti, *African Religions* 37-49; also see Mbiti's *Concepts of God in Africa*.

Of greater importance, however, is the fact that Beatrice taught that Christ appeared as a Black man in São Salvado and that all apostles were black.[17]

The tendency to color God black recurs in a broad base of Christian Black religious thought. To live, to exist as a particular being, means to be a creature of a God, and to be at a given point in God's creation. A religious person attempts to bring God into the arena of his or her life's social, economic, and political settings, because at such points one needs and meets and worships a God. In the personal arena of existence, one's very being can be addressed and authenticated only by God. Everyone colors God in the hues of relevancy, no less so Black people.

In the 1920s Marcus Garvey was hailed as a Black Moses because he stirred Black people with the promises of the Universal Negro Improvement Association. As a result of Garvey's emphasis on the blackness of God—revealed in the blackness of his son, Jesus Christ—black Madonnas and carvings of black Christs began to appear in many sections of the country.

In another historical context, in response to the question, "What is the color of God?" George Alexander McGuire Camp answered this way:

> A spirit has neither color nor natural parts nor qualities. But do we not speak of His hands, His eyes, His arms and other parts? Yes, it is because we are able to think and speak of God only in human and figurative terms.
> If, then, you have to think or speak of the color of God, how would you describe it? As a Black person, since we are created in His image and likeness, on what would you base your assumption that God is Black? On the same basis as that taken by White people when they assume that God is of their color.[18]

God's inferential blackness appeared nowhere more eloquently than in Countee Cullen's "Black Christ." In another poem, "The Heritage," Cullen offered the following lines, deeply expressive of the collective desire of many Black people who consider the Christian faith.

> My conversion came high-priced;
> I belong to Jesus Christ. . . .
> Lamb of God, although I speak
> With my mouth, thus, in my heart

---

[17]David J. Bosch, "Current and Cross-Currents in South African Black Theology," *Journal of Religion in Africa* 6:1 (1974).

[18]George Alexander McGuire Camp, *Universal Negro Catechism* (Universal Negro Improvement Association, 1921) 3.

> Do I play a double parr
> Wishing he I served were Black. . . .[19]

With the advent of contemporary Black Theology, writers raised the question of the color of God in relation to his character. Explorations of this relationship are Albert B. Cleage, Jr.'s *The Black Messiah*[20]and William R. Jones' *Is God a White Racist?*,[21]in which the question of color is raised in direct relation to the moral character of God.

In all his books about Black Theology, Black Power, and Black Liberation, James Cone contends that "there is no place in Black Theology for a colorless God. Especially is this true in a society where Black people suffer precisely because of their color." This is so, because God has made the goal of Black people to be his own goal. "Black Theology believes that it is not only appropriate," Cone argues, "but necessary to begin the doctrine of God with the insistence on his blackness."[22]

J. Deotis Roberts puts the color of God in another but similar perspective.

> Could not the blackness of the Black Messiah be a type of hiddenness and yet revealedness of God, as Barth would put it? If God in the Incarnate Word comes as man and if the Prince comes (as Brunner says) in beggar's garments, is it not conceivable that He comes to the Black man in his blackness? Is the concept of God as being incognito, in the Word made Flesh, off limits to the Black experience? Isn't it possible that God addresses each man and each people where they are in his/their human situation in a manner that is redemptive? These are ideas bandied about by theologians. May not Black theologians try them on for size? Our problem centers around what Christ can mean to Christians in Black skins in a racist society.[23]

Blacks relate God's color to his moral character because they are coming to terms with their blackness while still living within an unethically pro-White host culture. Many Black people wonder if God himself has accepted the White

---

[19]Countee Cullen, "The Heritage," in *On Thee I Stand* (1949; rpt., New York: Harper and Row, 1953) i, stanzas 5 and 6.

[20]Albert B. Cleage, Jr., *The Black Messiah* (New York: Sheed and Ward, 1968).

[21]William R. Jones, *Is God a White Racist?* (Garden City, NY: Anchor Press, 1973).

[22]James H. Cone, *A Black Theology of Liberation* (Philadelphia: J. B. Lippincott Company, 1970) 121.

[23]J. Deotis Roberts, "Black Theology and the Theological Revolution," *Journal of Religious Thought* 30:1 (Spring-Summer 1973): 16.

meaning of blackness in its most degrading sense. The White Christian church, which so glibly proclaims his Word, has not fully and forthrightly addressed itself to the problems of being Black in White America.

Nevertheless, some Black people reject the trend to color God black, feeling that it is wrong to give God a color identity or to require color as a moral attribute. Such a trend, they say, is anthropomorphic, reductionist, and unworthy of theological consideration. However, taking an objective view of the history of God-concepts and a subjective view of the needs of Black people, one is moved to ask, "Why not?" Black people have a right to appropriate God in their own color, and to express the full palette of God's color in art forms, language symbols, and literature.

Seeing God's color is analogous to seeing God as female. The feminist tendency is to decry the sexist language in most traditional expressions of theology written by male theologians. One might ask in response, "Is it not in order for males to refer to God in terms that reflect their relatedness to God as beings?" Taking turns, one would hope that, rather than being overcritical of male theologians who use language pertinent to their gender, female theologians would address God as "She," in terms that authentically reflect how God relates to women as female beings. Moreover, because males have often been the oppressors of females, women have all the more reason to reconceptualize God in the light of how God relates to a female as a human being.

The issue, indeed, is not so much gender or color, but oppression. When the oppressed no longer accept the God of the oppressor, then the process of liberation has already begun. When an oppressed people become unwilling to accept any longer a religion or a God premised upon the idea of inequality in any part of the human family, a new degree of theological maturity has been achieved. Black Theology's reconceptualization of God has been rationalistic in approach, defining not only the notion of deity but also relating the concept of deity to the human struggle. Whether in the theological search for a usable interpretation of the concept of God or the worshipful faith in the Subject of that concept, Black art, Black literature, and Black language forms reflect the Black perception of God's character as related to his color.

On the other hand, even though Black Theology is liberating God from slavery to a White God-concept (and feminist theology is freeing God from a male-dominant God-concept), one must register a theological caveat. In refashioning God to the extent that the idea of God itself becomes identical with a God who is personally conceived, what becomes of the transcendent God who abides, an infinite and eternal being beyond all gender, inclusive of all colors? What Black person can afford to disagree with James Cone's assertion that "the Blackness of God means that God has made the oppressed condition his own condition . . . the Blackness of God . . . means the essence of the nature of God is to be found in the concept of liberation."[24] And yet, this tendency to color God Black, giving—as it does—explicit and implicit distinction to Black theological reflection, is characteristic of the tendency to interpret God and religion from too narrow a frame of reference. This, however, may well be part of our human limitations with which we must learn to live comfortably, while, at the same time, repenting.

The authentically Black God of Afro-American Black Theology has never been a totally transcedent deity, unrelated to a social cause, but a divinity imminent in the Black people's struggle for liberation and freedom. But then, religion for the Black church has never been merely theoretical and speculative; it has always been practical, as well. Has not the God of the Black religious experience had traditionally to distill and purify for us the dark experiences of brutal oppression? Thus, for the Black person, the search for God has never been simply an intellectual pastime; but rather, always the result of an inner and outward struggle pursued with great effort. In continuity with this struggle and search, the Black community is now seeking a living God more real to them, no longer tinted with the color of the oppressor.[25]

In relating the character of God to his color, one eventually comes to a critical question. Is it possible to conceive of God as White or Black or male or female without making God too narrow to be fully representative of the total human family, much less of that which is divine? All that we know in human beings is relative; but that which we conceive of as God must, or ought to be, normative. This is the inherent danger in representing God in a human form or describing God with any human characteristics, whether concrete or abstract. God is always more than one can know, because to identify with God is an act of faith which has deep moral implications. But people—especially "other" people—are always more than one can know, too; and to be able to identify with others in their otherness is also an act of faith with deep moral implications.

The "otherness" of Black people makes it all the more important for them to see the relevancy of God's otherness to them in their blackness; for, it is because of their blackness that they are where and who they are today in American culture. Deotis Roberts believes that "When the human condition and the self-awareness that makes [sic] the difference known to the one who experiences change, then what God is revealing . . . is understood in a different light. What God unveils of his purpose to the slum dweller must be redemp-

---

[24]James H. Cone, *A Black Theology of Liberation,* 121.

[25]Ibid., 401

tive to such a man where he is first, even if it also promises deliverance, as I believe it does.[26]

In a predominantly non-White world, where Black is more and more dramatically defined as "non-White," the idea of a merely White God is becoming theologically untenable, or, at best, inadequate. The mood of the liberation quest now gripping Black people's imagination the world over demands a God whose traits are closer to the African—not a set of White or pale Semitic traits drawn through the siphon of centuries of Caucasian culture. God has been perceived within the Black religious tradition as a dynamic power immanent and involved in the primary affairs of mankind. God for us has never been a reality totally removed from the world or uninvolved in the historical process. For the Black person of faith, God is, and always has been, Almighty both Transcendence and Immanence on the march and sitting-in. James Baldwin spoke as strongly as any Black theologian could have spoken when he reminded us that the whole history of Afro-American Black people within the host culture has been troubled by an inadequate concept of what God is.

> From my point of view, this concept is not big enough. It has got to be made much bigger than it is because God is, after all, not anybody's toy. To be with God is really involved with some enormous, overwhelming desire and joy, and power which you cannot control, which controls you. I conceive of my own life as a journey toward something I do not understand, which in the going toward, makes me better. I conceive God, in fact, as a means of liberation and not a means to control others.[27]

Currently in Black literature, both non-theological and religious, a groping is apparent for an even newer concept of God. This relevant, living God is a God of revolution, who relates to the aspirations of the oppressed. In some people's minds, a desire burns to "kill the White God," so that the God of the Black people can make his presence known.[28]

In an opposite direction, Leroi Jones is an example of a Black, non-religious literary figure. James Baldwin, however, expresses a synthesis between the religious and the nonreligious in his writings, and he reflects the maturing reconceptualization of God which I have in mind. Baldwin bridges the gap

---

[26]J. Deotis Roberts, *Liberation and Reconciliation: A Black Theology* (Philadelphia: Westminster Press, 1971) 79.

[27]James Baldwin, *Nobody Knows My Name* (New York: Dell Publishing Co., 1969) 113.

[28]James H. Cone, *A Black Theology of Liberation* (New York: Lippincott Company, 1970) 114ff.

between radical realism and radical faith. In *Tell Me How Long the Train's Been Gone,* Baldwin's character, Leo Proudhammer, reflects on his inability any longer to accept the "White God" of the Black religion: "I had had quite enough of God—more than enough—the horror filled my nostrils; I gagged on the blood-drenched name; and, yet, was forced to see that this horror precisely accomplished His reality and un-did my belief."[29] Baldwin's Proudhammer could reject the old God, but he could not put off the new one—the one who transcends the old one, who assumes him and discards him in the passing of an era. God is there in the very metaphysics of all human aspiration, struggle, suffering, and even feeling a sense of guilt. One can never quite dismiss God. Baldwin would have us conclude that one can only hope to grow up to the fullness of being what is possible when one turns to God.

Both the religious and nonreligious literature of the dark days before and after slavery, prior to the Black Revolution of the sixties and the later seventies, is filled with the Black labor to unbelieve and rebelieve in God. W.E.B. Du Bois may well have caught, all in a few words, all the struggle to believe in God in spite of God.

> Keep not thou silent, O God!
> Sit no longer blind, Lord God, deaf to our prayer
> And dumb to our dumb suffering. Surely Thou, too,
> are not White, O Lord, a pale, bloodless, heartless thing.[30]

---

[29]James Baldwin, *Tell Me How Long the Train's Been Gone* (New York: Dell Publishing Company, 1969) 160.

[30]W. E. B. Du Bois, *Dark Water* (New York: Harcourt, Brace and Howe, 1920) 175-76.

CHAPTER FOUR

The Hermeneutics of Black Theology's Afro-Americanized God-Concept

THE HERMENEUTICAL TASK

Current expressions of Black Theology include hermeneutical constructs by which the conception of God and the world are defined according to the Black religious experience. Scripture, sermons, oral accounts of faith, story, song, and folklore are incorporated with traditional and contemporary experiences of social, political, and economic struggle, all this grasped in the light of modern methods of critical assessment. An informed Black theologian must acknowledge a God who prizes Black people's history of pain and celebration, present existence, and particularly their striving for freedom and love.

A usable concept of a personal God in the Afro-American religious experience must rest upon realistic ideas that relate his revelatory activities to the life and experiences of the people addressed by him within their particular history. As James H. Cone says, "Black Theology's view of God must be sharply distinguished from the many White distortions about God.[1] . . . Only Black people can speak about God as He is related to . . . their Black condition."[2] God becomes a living reality to Black people as they appropriate this concept existen-

---

[1]James H. Cone, *A Black Theology of Liberation* (Philadelphia. J. D. Lippincott Company, 1970) 117.

[2]Ibid.

tially in terms of understanding of what "God" means personally. In no other way, and upon no other assumptions, can the goodness of God be made intelligible in a world of imperfection, horror, and human suffering.

BASIC CRITERIA
FOR AN AFRO-AMERICANIZED CONCEPT
OF THE PERSONAL GOD

The first criterion for belief in a God who is usable within the Afro-American religious experience is the need to be able to say that "God is." To say "God is" is to assert without any rationally or otherwise supportive argument that there is a God. Because God's ontological is-ness is God's very nature, everything else exists in relation to God. God is the Being itself of all other beings: God is our reality. God's is-ness is ultimate, because God is the beginning and the end, "the Alpha and the Omega" (Rev. 1:8). God alone is self-existent, free from all dependence on any other external being and from any limitation by other forces. This means that the ground and ultimate explanation of God's being is within his radically free, wholly independent, self-existing self. This can be said of no other ontological being; for, all others— God only excepted—are in some way dependent on another. Anselm had this concept of God in mind when he said that God is "that than which nothing greater can be conceived." But because, moreover, God's existential reality formally and efficiently defines God's character and nature, Black Theology is not content merely to affirm *that* God is or *what* God is; Black Theology must go beyond Anselm and affirm *who* God is, also.

The second criterion for belief in a usable God in the Black theological tradition is the affirmation that God is a personal being. Not only is God the supreme and ultimate source of all reality emanating from himself alone but also God is that being of goodness and love who fundamentally upholds the world, because he wants to, for his own good pleasure, and for the world's good. Of God alone can one speak of a self-existent, absolute reality who is also a good and loving person.

Historian of theology John Macquarrie, without fully accepting personalism, acknowledged that God is a personal being, because

> personal being is the most appropriate symbol for being itself; for personal being stands highest in the hierarchy of beings which all seek to be like God. Personal being, as showing the richest diversity in unity and the highest possibilities for creativity and love, gives to our minds the fullest disclosure of the mystery of being that we can receive.[3]

---

[3]John Macquarrie, *Principles of Christian Theology* (New York: Charles Scribner's Sons, 1966) 250.

Black Theology affirms that only in God's divine being do we meet true personhood (or personality). Because the personal God is the cause of all existence, it follows that God is the source of all personal values—"values," by definition, being derived exclusively from persons. Only the absolute and absolutely personal God has the right to say in an unqualified way: "I am who I am—I will be whatever I will be." Black Theology therefore affirms that the absolutely personal God extends to other persons, created in his image and according to his likeness, the radical freedom and independent wholeness that comes with personal existence derived from dependence upon the Self-existent Power of Love and Goodness, whom we name God.

To explain why in the Black theological tradition we affirm without apology the absolute personhood of God, it might be helpful to distinguish three different views of the absolute.

The agnostic view of the absolute generally affirms the absolute, but declares that God, in his absolute personhood, is beyond the reach of theoretical knowledge. Immanuel Kant, and to some extent Spencer, represent this external-to-God point of view. The Book of Ecclesiastes (7:24) expresses this pious agnosticism when the author reminds us that God is to be conceived as "that which is far off and exceedingly deep; who can find it out?"

The impersonalist view of the absolute affirms the absolute as the highest possible universal quality, as the sum of all being, as something currently actual and potentially futural, an existing Reality yet to be fully realized. As God, the ultimate Being itself takes up into and surmounts in the unity of being all possible distinctions and differences. This idea is found in Hegel, in pantheism, and in certain expressions of Process thought. Whenever the absolute is conceived in any sense as being personal, it is transcendent of all that we can conceptualize in ordinarily personal terms.

The personalist view conceives of an absolute being both spiritually infinite and naturally personal, who is the creator and the sustaining power of all reality. This view is dominated by the category of causality; therefore, the absolute is conceived as the personal creative force underlying all reality. While such a personal being is the source of all reality, it is not equated with that created reality. God transcends the reality for which he is creatively responsible.

The most reasonable view for a Black theologian is the personalist understanding of the absolute. The first-mentioned points of view are not useful, because they fail to give to the absolute personal God his quality of being independent and self-existent. In Process thought, God is too contiguous to his created processes to be truly independent; and agnosticism says it doesn't know. To the extent of excluding quasi-personalist views, the Black theologian must be clear that God is the independent ground and self-existent cause of all other causes or being precisely as a personal—not an impersonal—being. God's creation is thus not a part of his own personal being, but is, rather, the expression of or the consequence of God's creative activity—an effect, which, as such proves God's personhood to be distinguishable from its results. In a related sense, however, God is self-limiting limitations freely taken on due to the limitedness of his creatures. Methodist Bishop Francis McConnell instructed us on this difficult point when he said that: (1) "If we are to think about God at all, we must think of him as being under some sort of self-limitation" on account of the nature of his creation. (2) In a derogatory sense of the term, "the unlimited God of abstract thought is more limited than the Christian self-limited God. . . . It is the abstract theologians who limit God." Indeed, "the movement away from the [personally] concrete toward the [impersonally] abstract is itself a kind of limitation."[4]

The final, Black theological criterion needed for a usable concept of God must be the affirmation that the God who is, who is personal, and who is creatively free and independent, good and loving in his personhood, is also an ultimately responsive being. A personally responsive God-concept is deeply woven into the fabric of the Black church. From beginning to end, the Bible teaches that God, the personal, living, creating God, is not simply the first principle of reality, the sustainer of the universe and the mere cosmic process but also that God is pervasive love, the rectifier of moral order, the evaluator of values. God, the ultimate in personableness, is no mere system of ideals, but a responsive personal being who cares. God is the one who always relates and responds in love; therefore, God is the one who wills us ultimately only good.

THE HERMENEUTICS OF BLACK PERSONALISM

To say that God is personal and caring is not to equate God solely with the conceptualized personal as we know personhood within the limitations of our human experience. To conceive of the living God as personal is to conceive of God as being the Ultimate Person who knows and cares about all aspects of creation. To say that God is personal is to see God both as caring about and identifying with the whole creation, and as caring about each one of us. The Ultimate Person's "eye is on the sparrow," as we sing; and that he knows each member of the human family—even you and me. If God did not know us personally and individually, personal religious faith would not be valid. As a Black theologian, one must affirm God as a personal being with a positive response to the question: "Does God care about each one of us on this earth?" If God is not a personal, consciously caring being, who knows each one of us intimately enough to be concerned about what happens to every one of us, then God has no relevancy for our individual faith.

---

[4]Francis J. McConnell, *Is God Limited?* (New York: Abingdon Press, 1924) 17ff.

Affirmation of God as a personal living being is affirmation of the biblical, Hebrew God-concept. The functions ascribed to God in the Bible could not have been carried out by a nonpersonal, absolute ideal or a mere process. No non-personal or sub-personal deity would be worthy of fellowship, worship, faith, or following. Only a personal God could have identified with the liberating needs of Israel in Egypt and the ongoing Jewish struggle for social, economic, and political justice. Black people worship a God like that.

The God of the Black community of faith must be a living God, personally active in creation. Every affirmation of faith must include a statement of both the nearness and remoteness of God. When Black believers speak of God as a living personal being, they confess the activity of God as an expression of the divine will to maintain a spiritual and personal relationship with every human person and, indeed, with every particle of God's creation.

Theistic personalism for the Black church means more than just God's "aseity,"—the technical term in metaphysics that refers to God's self-caused existence. The Black theologian includes in the term "God" an idea of absolute personal perfection. Consequently, the divine absoluteness manifests itself in three different realms: the metaphysical, the cognitive, and the ethical, each of which is essential to a full understanding of the Black person's God-concept.

The Black theologian speaks metaphysically of God as the ultimate personal category of being-itself. God is the supreme person, the only self-possessing selfhood. Really, we could not conceive of God as being otherwise. Black personalism contends that "to be" is to be a "self." By a self, Black personalism means that God is a unitary, self-identifying, conscious agent. As the ultimate category of being-itself, we see God as the only supremely conscious being standing in relation to everyone who exists and everything that happens.

This affirmation of God as a personal living being, however, provokes the cognitive question—the question of how we know God. Do we know God's person by being acquainted with the divine Self itself? Or, do we know the divine Person only in terms of God's being called a person in relation to us? Or is the true personhood of God's divine self hidden from us? Karl Rahner struggles with this question in his reference to God as one thought of in "absolute and transcendent distance." But Rahner overcomes this potential cognitive breakdown by remaining consistently personalistic; he reasonably argues that God is personal simply because it is inconceivable to think of God as alive and possessing less than infinite personhood. How could that which is itself less than personal call that which is personal into being?

The notion that the absolute ground of all reality is something like an unconscious and impersonal cosmic law, an unconscious and impersonal structure of things, a source which empties itself out without possessing itself, which gives rise to spirit and freedom without itself being spirit and freedom; the notion of a blind, primordial ground of the world which cannot look at us even if it wants to, all of this is a notion whose model is taken from the context of the impersonal world of things. It does not come from that source in which a basic transcendental experience is rooted; namely, from a finite spirit's subjective and free experience of itself.[5]

By its very constitution, a finite spirit experiences itself as having its origins in another and as having been given to itself from another. Therefore, it cannot misrepresent, misconceive, or misinterpret the other from which it derived its being as merely an impersonal principle. God must be personal; because, even if one were to assume that human life, human personality, and self-conscious human beings could have come from an impersonal source—as difficult as that simple assumption might be—one still must question whether an impersonal source could care as deeply for its creation as we believe God does. Evidence of this care we see in scriptures, songs, prayer and in worship.

Black personalism advances the contention that God is a responsive personal being who knows and cares about each one of us, while ever maintaining—with Rahner—the cognitive humility required by the dark truth of God's personhood, a truth that remains "true of God only if, in asserting and understanding this statement, we open it to the inevitable darkness of the holy mystery."[6] God's personhood is the ultimate category of being itself, and therefore beyond our full knowing. Black theologians insist that we know God not *inseipso*—not in the mystery of divine selfhood—but only as we allow God to become personal to us can we hope to encounter God as God seeks to encounter us. This takes place in the depths of our individual consciousness and in the whole history of the human race.

Black Theology further confesses that in the personhood of Jesus Christ can we see God as incarnate Word coming to us in God's own way of self-communication different from the whole of human history and the individual religious experience. But again, a perceptive Black theologian speaking to the Black church could not possibly conceive of Jesus Christ as God's incarnate Word coming into our history as anything less than the fully personal expression of the God who is supremely personal. A Black theologian would agree with the German Catholic Rahner that "God's self-communication means, therefore, that what is communicated is really God in his own [personal] 'being.' " Jesus Christ is God's act of communication for the sake of the hu-

---

[5]Karl Rahner, *Foundations of Christian Faith: An Introduction to the Idea of Christianity,* trans. William V. Dych (New York: Seabury Press, 1978) 75.

[6]Ibid., 74.

man knowing and possessing God in "immediate vision and love."[7] (I discuss Jesus below in chapter seven; I mention him here as the clearest expression of God's personhood.)

It is in the ethical dimension, however, that theological Black personalism must radically distinguish itself from White theistic personalism. God is conceived by the theological Black tradition as being a responsive personal being with unquestioned, and unlimited, absolute power. No authentic Black theologian, male or female, could embrace a God-concept limited to the interests of a ruling ethnic class, however triumphant. That would be a truly weak God, incapable of taking sides with his oppressed people. We must ask: *What weak, oppressed people could afford to worship a weak God?* The God of the Black church, the God of liberation, the God of freedom struggles, and the God of ultimate salvation surely must be morally absolute and ethically unlimited. We cannot doubt that God is ever in complete control of creation and that, ultimately, his ethical triumph over all evil forces will be complete.

THE MORAL CHARACTER
OF THE AFRO-AMERICANIZED GOD

The symbols or analogies through which Black theologians conceive of God as being supremely personal are best clarified by relating the divine attributes to the ethical completeness of God's holy personhood. We can approach the task of assessing divine integrity by studying the moral character of the Black God.

Personality and moral quality are the most human and valuable attributes of divine nature. Without a moral quality, the idea of a personal God would be of little value for a personal faith, especially within the Black religious experience. Personality and moral quality are conspicuous attributes of God in both the Old and the New Testaments. God's personhood in the Scriptures has as its essential elements moral selfhood, moral self-consciousness, moral self-control, and the absolute power to be, to do, and to know. The following list of God's discrete moral attributes is merely an attempt to explain the ethical dimensions of God's absolute holy personal being. These attributes coinhere within the unity of God's personhood as a collective of characteristics, just as the several aspects of human character coexist within the integrated personality of any individual.

Because of its emphasis on personhood, first in the hierarchy of God's personal qualities to be mentioned as essential for Black theology is the *unity of*

---

[7]Ibid., 117-18.

God: God is one. As a holy, personal, active being of will and power, God is neither multiple nor composite, not to be conceived of as a plurality of Gods or ever thinkably at odds within the divine self. The ultimate of all personal beings, God neither differentiates the divine self into lesser beings nor manifests the divine presence through the creature. Although there be other invisible spiritual powers, the Lord is the highest God and alone worthy of the name "God." No other God or Gods of equal quality or status of being exist (Deut. 6:4). God has no equals, as might be the case were one to consider God literally as a "he" or a "she."

Whereas the unity of God defines what is formally required for God to be God—that God be absolutely one in personhood—the fundamentally efficient requirement is the *absolute power of God*. In the fullest sense, the uniqueness of God is exampled most decisively in God's absolute power "to be" and "to let be," "to exist" and "let exist," "to act" and "to move others to act," and "to will" and "to will others to will." No other person has this absolute power, totally free and utterly independent. God alone is unlimited in the power to be.

The question that addresses the power of God most pointedly is some form of the question asked by William R. Jones: "Is God a White Racist?" Black Theology asks not so much the question of what God has the power to do, but whether Black people can get God to use the divine power on their behalf. The central question in the Black religious experience is not "Does God exist?" but "Does God care?" Black people have perforce related to God out of the condition of their having been oppressed. Human needs, however, cry out for a dependable power both adequate to meet those needs and friendly enough to be disposed towards caring about human need. Divine power and human need go together in an equation in which mutual divine and human love is the third operator. God's power and God's love are equally important in Black religious thought, and equally related to how God is viewed. Power was the distinctive divine attribute according to both Jewish and African religions; and Jesus declared that "God cares" and demonstrated that "God is love." What, then, Black people ask, is the use or value of a God who loves, but is powerless to act? How could we worship a God too deficient in power to implement love? How could we love a God too deficient in love to give power its caring focus. Void of power as absolute as God's love is said to be, God would find little following in the Black community.

God as one and powerful and personal is addressed in the Black religious experience as *a spiritual being*. As a unitary spiritual being, God is worshiped as distinct from any material or physical existent or as any mere ideal or operative process. As spiritual, God is one: God is non-complex, and therefore transcends every material concept. As a powerful spiritual being, God is free from the weaknesses of flesh. Supramundane in spiritual vigor, more than a material body, superior to the forces of nature and to nature in all its created powers, God is simply more than we can limit with our knowing. As a personal spiritual being, the innermost depth and the essential moral nature of God is to be espied by the faithful eye. Supernatural goodness lies at the very core of God's being, and it is this supernatural goodness that makes God supremely personal.

This first cluster of divine attributes—God's oneness, God's power, and God's spirituality—is summarized in Black Theology by the affirmation that *God is a personal being of perfect holiness.* To say that God is holy is to assert that God is outside all evil and to affirm that God's ethical perfection excludes from the divine personality all tendencies toward or any delight in evil. Whereas we understand that God's mind comprehends evil, we are certain that evil finds no echo in the divine sensibility and no realization in the divine will. Positively stated, this means that God delights only in good, that God is devoted solely to goodness, and that in God's personal holiness the concept of moral perfection is wholly realized.

This first cluster of divine attributes, further, refers primarily to God within the divine self (God *ad intra*), God within himself prior to any relationship with creatures. Black Theology, however, is a practical theology interested mostly in a usable God; therefore, Black religion pays homage principally to God in his relationship to creatures (God *ad extra*). God's personal and moral perfections, however, translate directly into two theological categories that dominate Black theological ethics: *the omnipotence of God and God's righteousness.* It is God the transcendent Omnipotent, we believe, who cannot be assailed by the evil that has befallen us; and it is God the Righteous to whom we pray in his lordship over history, ruling and moving absolutely on behalf of his oppressed Black people.

In both the Old and New Testaments, God is identified with the moral principle of the universe, a principle, moreover, that is held to be absolutely sovereign. God is always and without exception, therefore, committed to the ultimate and positive good of his creation. He is by nature opposed to all evil, against which his wrath is ever directed. To comprehend God in a way that corresponds to his nature, one must "know" through the intimate union of joining with him in his omnipotent cosmic action on behalf of the righteousness of justice and love.

Omnipotence and ethics have ever been radically fused throughout the whole of the Black religious tradition. A sense of "what ought to be" has persisted in Black religious thoughts, even when things were not as they ought to have been. Many years after slavery, David Walker, thinking about slavery, could still say that "God Almighty will tear up the face of the earth."

Martin Luther King, Jr., told of the early days of civil rights activities when he was gripped by a paralyzing fear for his life and the security of his family. At one time, Dr. King confessed that he had thought to get out of the struggle; but, being a child born in the Black religious tradition, he took those deep concerns to God. Then, one night in prayer, God appeared to Dr. King:

> At that moment I experienced the presence of the Divine as I had never before experienced him. It seemed as though I could hear the quiet assurance of an inner voice, saying: "Stand up for righteousness, stand up for truth. God will be at your side forever." Almost at once my fears began to pass from me. My uncertainty disappeared. I was ready to face anything. The outer situation remained the same, but God had given me inner calm.[8]

The sense of "what ought to be" was the driving spirit of King's theological orientation and ethical action. In private and public this was his obsession. The all-powerful God was, for him, at one with justice and love. King's view was then and still is the central theme of Black theological ethics—the primordial identity of justice, power, and love.

The Almighty relates to all sides of social issues, but in radically different ways. Divine Love takes the deliberate risk of entering into relation at all levels with his creatures at every point in human history. As one who cares, divine Justice grapples with every human experience, exposing himself to the pain of his creation, the possible rejection, the suffering, and even the Cross. Divine Power assures a positive end.

This dimension of the divine attributes through which God turns towards the creature—God's onmipotence and God's righteousness—is pondered by Black people of faith in religious awe at *the God of love who is also the God of wrath.* More than any other attribute, the love of God expresses the positive divine relatedness to creation. This concept is the answer to the question: "Is the universe friendly?"—a question which gets asked frequently, since the dying universe, bloodthirsty nature, and heartless human history—all of them, creations of the God of wrath—have so often behaved in so unfriendly a way towards Black people.

At the heart of this question lies the basis of religion. This is the question to which the Scriptures, taken as a whole, give a positive answer: According to the Scriptures, "Yes, the universe is friendly, because God is love!" God always relates to his people in love: Even in his wrath and righteous judgement God's love is expressed. God hates the sin, but he loves the sinner. He stands not in the splendid isolation of glorious holiness as the "unmoved

---

[8]Martin Luther King, Jr., *Strength to Love* (New York: Harper and Row, 1963) 107.

mover"; neither does he remain beyond and above all essence and existence, aloof in the untarnished and perfect unity of the plenteous one. God becomes real to us by being responsive. And yet, even God's love is exacting in what it requires of his creation, and wrathful in its righteousness when a creature offends against justice and love. James H. Cone, discussing the wrath or righteousness of God in relation to the love of God, contends that although the theological statement, "God is love," is the most acceptable assertion regarding the nature of God, it has been misused to exclude an understanding of the wrath or righteousness of God in relation to that divine love. Cone rejects the tendency of most modern-day White theologians, who assert God's love to the total neglect or exclusion of his wrath. Cone would interpret the love of God in the light of his wrath: "It is not possible to understand what God's love means for the oppressed without making *wrath* an essential ingredient of that love. . . . Most theological treatments of God's love fail to place the proper emphasis on God's wrath, suggesting that love is completely self-giving without any demand for obedience."[9]

Cone contends further that a God of love, denuded of divine wrath, does not plan to do much liberating: The two concepts, love and wrath, belong together. "A God minus wrath seems to be a God who is basically not against anybody. All we have to do is behave nicely, and everything will work out all right. But such a view of God leaves us in doubt about God's role in the Black-White struggle. Black people want to know what or whose side God is on and what kind of decision He is making about the Black Revolution."[10]

Whereas Cone is right to understand God as a God of both love and wrath, Cone is unclear on how God applies his wrath when fused with his love; and in this sense, Cone neglects the ethical character of God. Certainly, the justice of God is exacting and direct in its opposition to wrong; and God loves even those against whom his wrath is directed. But the connecting link between God's wrathful justice and his suffering love is his omnipotent redemption. God is not on anyone's side, right or wrong. He is against any wrong actions and for anything perfective of his creation. God takes all sides and applies his love or his wrath in balance as needed. Contrary to the usual human sense, God transcends all sides. Deotis Roberts expressed a balanced Black view of divine justice this way: "All power is a precious attribute of God for Black people; for them impotent goodness has little appeal . . . a God who is ab-

---

[9]Cone, *A Black Theology of Liberation,* 130-31.

[10]Ibid.

solute in both power and goodness makes sense to Black men. . . . Absolute goodness insures us that absolute power will not be abused."[11]

It is evident that Afro-American Black people have a vested interest in what ought to be. The means which has most often and most effectively been available to them for achieving that ideal has been religion. In a consideration of Black religion in its relationship to the attributes of God discussed thus far, we come to a third constellation of divine qualities made especially clear in the Black religious experience. As Cecil W. Cone says, because religion was "the whole system of being" for the Africans who were brought to this country, "it is only natural that religion would be the primary means by which they would attempt to cope with their condition, as well as the weapon for opposing that condition."[12]

The deep need to survive explains the central role that religion played in the slaves' struggle and endurance. Human beings need more than merely physical or mental power to endure and survive. The survival faith of Afro-American Blacks is still very much alive today. It seems strange that a people so deprived of justice and oppressed by power could believe so deeply in the power and justice of God. But it is precisely this religious belief, lying authentically and deeply in the Afro-American concept of God as a God of justice and wrath, that countervailed against their experience of raw injustice. Because of human injustice, Black people have sought in a just God the divine counter to all injustice. If Black people could not have believed in a God as just as he is loving, as righteous as he is omnipotent, they could not have believed in God at all.

The God of Black religious piety and Christian devotion is *a God of grace,* a God of mercy, and a God of self-restraint. God's love relating to his people presupposes a positive quality in God's responsive movement towards his people, even towards those who actively rebel against him. Towards human rebellion, "God's arms are stretched out still." Grace is God's free movement towards human beings who have turned away from him. Grace is that sobering qualification of God's omnipotence and holiness which makes it possible for the most sinful person to trust him. God's grace is "prevenient," that is, it reaches out from God's dread hiddenness and awesome differentness to make possible the timid and fearful decisions such as people are able to make that are the beginnings of life in faith and love. Without God's prevenient

---

[11]J. Deotis Roberts, *Liberation and Reconstruction* (Philadelphia: Westminster Press, 1971) 88.

[12]Cecil W. Cone, *The Identity Crisis in Black Theology* (Nashville: The African Methodist Episcopal Church Press, 1974) 31.

grace—a free act on his part entirely independent of the foreseen merits or demerits of the individual—human beings would only mire themselves deeper in bondage to self. God's grace makes us free at last and gives us the ability in freedom to say "yes" or "no" to God.

No matter how strong a person is, nor how self-assertive and arrogant; no matter how long persons have been seeking to establish their own self-centered, self-ordered lives, nor how actively they may defy the God who "lets be"—God's mercy still lets them be. God's mercy is the opportunity for personal freedom; for God in mercy does not destroy or forsake persons because they exercise their human freedom. God's mercy is faithful, in that God will not let us go; but God's mercy lets one "be," even perversely and in spite of one's self. There is no human measure in such mercy; there are no extremes beyond which it will not go. God's grace and mercy are best understood through the symbol of the Cross. Through God's suffering on the Cross, inflicted upon him by human beings, God's grace hopes to win over the hearts of people in spite of themselves. Though God's power is absolute, God mercifully restrains himself when dealing with human beings. Through the loving self-restraint of God's power, we experience the grace and mercy of divine persuasion at its supremely mature level. This is a God who is all-powerful, restraining himself to deal with powerless creatures by means of love's power of persuasion only. Nikolai Berdyaev—who was not a Black theologian—argued this point best.

> God the creator . . . is powerless by self-restraint, to conquer evil by an act of power. It is only by means of sacrifice and self-identification with the human condition in love that God seeks to triumph over evil, the God who took upon himself the sins of the world. It was in a self-limiting love that the God who came in Jesus Christ, seeks, by this means, to win the hearts of human beings. In Jesus Christ, God establishes a new relationship with human beings. It is sometimes by means of "powerless love" that God wins or persuades human beings to himself. God is self-powerless to use his absolute power on powerless human beings.[13]

Divine self-restraint, nevertheless, does not rule out divine coercive justice, which makes demands upon the lives of persons who are loved and may be just the act of prevenient grace needed to free a rebellious one to say "yes" to God's justice. Love is fused with justice and therefore is not passive. It can be coercive and direct, is always compelling, and persuades by the power of example showing us what we could and should be.

---

[13]Nikolai Berdyaev, *The Beginning and the End* (New York: Macmillan, 1952) 248.

The divine self-restraint manifests itself further in a trinity of three other godly characteristics: *God's responsiveness, God's faithfulness, and God's forgiveness.* The faithfulness of God denotes his steadfast loyalty and relatedness to his creation. God's love for his creation so binds him to us until nothing can separate him from us or us from him. God remains faithful to us, even when we are unfaithful to him; and this means that he will never let his willful, contrary, errant creation go. Because God never gives up, we can trust God with the future.

God's faithfulness means more than that God can be relied on to keep on going his own impersonal way. God's faithfulness is also responsive to his people on terms that make sense to them. The Black church has been a groaning, praying, singing church, a church that poured out its needs to God in prayer. And then, because it has been a listening and waiting church, the Black church discovered that God is unconditionally committed to respond to his people's needs, that he answers their prayers, that he cares for them. This means that we may call on God in sheer belief, the fullness of faith, and the certainty of knowledge that God will respond. In the Black religious tradition, we believe that God will act.

Divine forgiveness proceeds out of the same righteousness and omnipotence that empower God's justice and wrath, and creates a parallel effect in anyone who stands under it. The human experience of estrangement between and restoration of persons is the symbol for our reunion with God, from whom we once were alienated and totally estranged. Forgiveness of another presupposes a full and complete recognition of the seriousness of the other's offense. If one who is forgiven thinks that the forgiving person is ignorant of the prior offense, guilt might well hang just as heavy after the act of forgiveness as it did before. The act of forgiving demands, therefore, that one give up any thought of reparations measured by the extent of the other's offense. Forgiveness offers itself freely, even with an absolute knowledge of the other's wrong. The guilty party may then rely on true forgiveness in the other, because the other's knowledge of the extent of the guilty one's offense makes forgiveness full and evident. When one is forgiven by God, one can be assured that God had absolute knowledge of the wrong. God forgives us anyway, with a forgiveness as complete and absolute as his knowledge and understanding of our wrongs.

Black Theology is right in its observation that the encounter with God in the Black religious tradition has had profound implications for the oppressed.[14] Attempting to sort out right from wrong, both within the Black community and beyond themselves in the host culture, Black people looked

---

[14]Cone, *A Black Theology of Liberation,* 107ff.

to God as the fixed ethical point of reference to help them overcome vacillation and shifting trends. [15] God alone has provided Black people with the ultimate definition of their humanity and a full sense of the ethical. [16] Black people's inner recognition of this definition of their being from within and beyond informed them that even the most adverse external climate in the host culture would eventually be changed by God himself. Therefore, always attempting to balance doubt with faith, Black believers have felt the need to struggle to become what God's call demanded them to become. Their view of what God wanted for them was always different from the host culture's view.

James Cone's description may somewhat oversimplify and overstate the outward appearance of the Black worship experience, but he correctly understands that it was their religion that led Black people on towards the radical change within and without that the God of Black Theology promised them:

> Black people, who have been humiliated and oppressed by the structures of White society for six days of the week, gather together each Sunday morning in order to experience another definition of their humanity. The transition from Saturday to Sunday is not just a chronological change from the seventh to the first day of the week. It is, rather, a rupture in time, a kairos—an event that produces a radical transformation in the people's identity. . . . Every person becomes "somebody" and one can see the people's recognition of their new-found identity by the way they stand and walk and carry themselves. [17]

In spite of far-too-frequent evidence to the contrary that they would ever be "somebody" in this world, Black people kept on believing that God wanted individual ethical and religious changes, but changes in the administration of his justice in society, as well. Thus, they became "somebody" at church and waited on the *knowledge of God* to embody itself in their somebodiness for the perfecting of creation far beyond their ability to know or conceive. God's knowledge transcends human knowledge; God's understanding passes human understanding. But the Black church believed that God's knowledge of their human condition was as intimate and detailed as his willing relatedness to them

---

[15]Clifton H. Johnson, ed., *God Struck Me Dead: Religious Conversion Experiences and Autobiographies of Ex-Slaves* (Philadelphia: Pilgrim Press, 1969) ix.

[16]Cone, *The Identity Crisis in Black Theology,* 48.

[17]James H. Cone, "Sanctification and Liberation in the Black Religious Tradition," in *Sanctification and Liberation,* ed. Theodore Runyan (Nashville: Abingdon Press, 1981) 176-77.

was complete and absolute. They were still suffering and they did not know why; but God knew. In the history of the Black Afro-American religious experience, the faith was that God would someday free Black people of their awful conditions. That was the faith of Black people when they were in slavery, when they were oppressed after slavery, and it is still the faith of the Black community today.

CHAPTER FIVE

Theodicy
and the Moral Character of God

EVIL AND THE QUALITY OF CREATION

The late Carter G. Woodson, an early Black historian, once argued in *The Mis-Education of the Negro* that Western theology has been too inclined to fix on the benevolent character of God to the exclusion of any other aspect of divine nature. This has the consequence of interpreting God as active in human affairs only where good is present. Even if one accepts Woodson's approach, the question still arises as to what God is doing in evil times. Woodson answered that question by attributing both good and evil to God. Woodson believed that his understanding of godly evil would allay questions of religious doubt in the Black religious community by making God responsible for the creation of both good and evil.[1] To the contrary, Woodson's idea raises serious questions about God's character. Can a good God also be a God of evil? This is one of the main questions contemporary Black Theology is trying to answer.

If Black Theology is to comprehend God within the world in which Black people live, it must eventually ask Cone's question: "How do we dare speak of God in a suffering world, a world in which Blacks are humiliated because they are Black people?"[2] If Black Theology is to be relevant to Black people, if it is to affirm God's power and love expressed in his creation, then it must also address the problems of evil and how they are related to God's character.

---

[1](Washington: The Associated Publishers, 1933).

[2]James H. Cone, *A Black Theology of Liberation* (Philadelphia: J.B. Lippincott Company, 1970) 115.

The more Black Theology seeks to affirm God's goodness in the setting of Black human existence, the more difficult becomes the problem of evil.

Looking objectively at creation, we observe that God has created a world with structures that give rise to both good and evil. The goodness of God's world does not exclude prominent evil and includes potential for an improved order of creation. People, likewise,—even those professing religion—are also involved in God's creation, both for good and evil. A discussion merely of one or the other is not complete.

Black Theology's choice must then be between a no-God concept, if it excludes evil, or more a intelligible concept of God, if it is to meet the facts of the Black experience. Even though we accept the principles that God freely and consciously chose to create an imperfect world and that all of his ways toward human beings cannot be fully understood or adequately explained, still we find that we lack a definitive answer to the "why" of evil. It is realistic to expect that our answers will always lack a total adequacy in completely settling the question of why God created such a world as ours. Perhaps it follows that Christianity has meaning especially because we understand our situation so poorly and know how far we can and cannot go toward fully explaining the world as we experience it. In our search for God, Black Theology must take care that it find a realistic God who conceptually relates to the conditions surrounding Black people, whom God has caused to live within a creation that God himself has chosen against all other options. Woodson's question demands an answer: What kind of God is the God who has created such a world as ours? Surely God could have made other choices! But God created this world. Is this the best world possible? If we conclude that God is good, then we must conclude that his creation is good. Apart from the issues of color, anyone considering the character of God eventually comes around to pondering the human condition. To cope with the facts of Black people's dark experience in American culture, Black Theology must somehow affirm God's ultimate power and God's ultimate love and deal, at the same time, with what feels like the opposite. To do this, Black Theology must affirm a love that moves between two opposite sides of God as God relates to creation.

Nevertheless, all attempts to resolve the question of theodicy thus far, whether by Black or White theologians, have run to one of two extremes, either of which leaves the devout believer in an all-powerful, good God unsatisfied. In the words of Sontag and Roth:

> One of these two views is that God consciously and directly wills from eternity every instance of evil that our world contains. The other is the view that

God has chosen a world in which he merely permits some evil, but does not cause or directly will any evil to occur.[3]

In the absence of a satisfactory theodicy within traditional Christian thought, Black Theology must draw upon its own resources to answer the question for itself.

EVIL AND THE POWER OF GOD

Any discussion of theodicy begins with the related questions: Is God a God of absolute or limited goodness? Is God finite or infinite? Put the questions together, and you get theological problems. If God is absolutely good and infinite in power, why does evil exist? On the other hand, if God is finite, or limited, in what ways does evil limit his power? What can he do? What can he not do? Indeed, if one believes in an infinite God, the problem of evil assumes its most acute form. Black theologian William R. Jones stated the problem this way:[4] If God is omnipotent, omniscient, and omnibenevolent (all-powerful, all-knowing and all-good), why is there suffering or evil in the world? It was William Jones' pointed question: "Is God a White Racist?" that brought the problem of evil into focus within the Black Theological discussion, although Benjamin Mays' book, *The Negro's God*,[5] shows that the theodicy question did not arrive with William R. Jones.

The slave preacher's sermons, Black songs, and the prayers of Black people were full of questions about a good God and the evil of suffering. Black theological interest in theodicy is as old as the Afro-American religious experience itself. Belief in the infinite God, however, has been so fundamental in Black church tradition that persons of deep faith are usually shocked by the suggestion that God may not possess unlimited power, total wisdom, or absolute goodness. Most Black Christians have agreed with Western theology that limitations on the essential attributes of God are derogatory and unthinkable. Popular Black religious thought has generally agreed with the dominant formal theology on this point: If God is not the almighty, then he is not truly God. In Black religious belief as with most Christian theology, Black or White, God's infinity includes much more than absolute power, knowledge, and goodness; omnipresence for example, is "all, everything." In summary, the popular idea of God affirms the divine nature as Perfect Being, "all," "everything," an all-inclusive attribution of perfection implying the co-inherence of all other attributes.

---

[3]Frederick Sontag and John K. Roth, *The American Religious Experience* (New York: Harper & Row, 1972) 250.

[4]William R. Jones, *Is God a White Racist?* (Garden City NY: Anchor Press, 1973).

[5]Benjamin E. Mays, *The Negro's God* (New York: Atheneum Press, 1973).

However, all theology must consider answers to the questions posed by theodicy[6]—especially the problems each question has for Black Theology, and for all theology.

CURRENT ANSWERS TO THE THEODICY QUESTION

A Finite-Infinite Answer to the Theodicy Question

Edgar S. Brightman's widely influential theistic personalist idealism has been further developed by his student, Peter A. Bertocci. Brightman's major concept was his conviction that radical evil cannot be reconciled with divine omnipotence.[7] According to Brightman's view, God is limited by external, uncreated, unchosen factors within his own nature and ontological being. Of course, he is the source and ground of all creation; unbegun and unending in time, infinite in space and including all nature in his experience; unlimited in his knowledge, perfect in goodness and love; nevertheless—according to Brightman and Bertocci—God is limited in power. God is thus the finite-infinite controller of "the given." There is an alien facet to the "given," an element not within the scope of God's will; and yet, the " 'given' is eternal within the will of God." This combination of the uncreated laws of reason and of the equally uncreated disorderliness, pain, and suffering are, existentially speaking, a "surd." The "given" includes both the rational and nonrational aspects within God's ontological being.[8] The former consists of the norms of reason and other orderly values; the latter are processes in the divine consciousness that exhibit, by analogy with human experience, "all the ultimate qualities of sense objects (qualia), disorderly impulses and desires . . . and whatever in God is the source of surd evil."[9] The nonrational "given" is thus the retarded factor that resists the efforts of God's perfectly good will to order reality according to his rational and positive intent. Nevertheless, God and humankind are both personal and akin in that they are both in a continuous state of becoming, both seeking and finding new ways to advance cosmic creation toward the achievement of positive values and ultimate good.

---

[6]See John Hick, *Evil and the God of Love* (New York: Harper & Row, 1978) for a broad survey of the theodicy question.

[7]Edgar Sheffield Brightman, *The Problem of God* (New York: The Abingdon Press, 1930) 113.

[8]Cf. S. Paul Schilling, *God and Human Anguish* (New York: Abingdon Press, 1977) 241ff.

[9]Brightman, *The Problem of God,* 113ff.

"God is the Cosmic Person," Brightman concludes "whose will is controlled or governed by creative, patient will."[10] The personality of God, conceived as the supreme person, together with the sacredness of human personality express the true genius of the Christian religion. By locating evil within the ontological being of God, Brightman concedes that God's will cannot, as of now, overcome all of the recalcitrant elements in the nonrational "given." That is, God does not have absolute control over all those processes within God himself that might be compared to the sensory, affective, and emotional life of human beings. The hampering effects of these elements within God's personality is due to excess or non-disciplinary evil.[11] After considering several interpretations, both Brightman and Bertocci conclude that within God's ontological self there must be a "resistant given" that blocks and limits God's own immediate and full realization of all the good that God wills.[12] The cause of evil, the world's imperfections, and evil's persistence are expressions of God's limited powers, and, seemingly, lack of absolute ability to act. Evil is in the world because God is limited; the world was created imperfect and unfriendly; these conditions continue unchecked and uncontrolled because God is helpless, at the moment, to do anything about it.

Brightman and Bertocci seem to complicate the problem of evil and the concept of God's being, because their view places a good-evil dualism within the very personhood of God. This view is almost totally alien to Black Theological reflection.

A Finite-God Answer to the Theodicy Question

To William Jones, it is impossible to believe in an unlimited God without admitting logical or moral contradictions in his very ontological being. God is either not all-powerful, or God is not all-wise; God cannot be all good if he is a White racist. In Jones' view, the big question is this: If evil exists and God is all good, and if God has the power and wisdom to eliminate evil but fails to do so, how can he be judged to have a sincere concern for the absolute good? If God is omnibenevolent, then he must have some reason for withholding his power to overcome evil. Either that, or he has no power or wish to do so. What, then, is God's creative purpose? Jones concludes that either

---

[10]E. S. Brightman, *A Philosophy of Religion* (New York: Prentice-Hall, 1940) 336-37; and *Person and Reality* (New York: Ronald Press, 1958), edited after Brightman's death by Peter Anthony Bertocci and Jannette E. Newhall.

[11]Edgar Sheffield Brightman, *A Philosophy of Religion* (New York: Prentice-Hall, 1940) 534-98 (cf. 430-33).

[12]Ibid., chs. 5 and 7; also *Person and Reality*.

God is a White racist, or he would not have allowed the long enslavement and oppression of Black people. Either God is not omnipotent and omniscient, or else God is not good. If he were good, he would not have willed racism. Because God has allowed racism, he himself must be a White racist. We look at Jones' view again, below.

The doctrine of a limited God, as found in Jones' view and others, has been derived from many honest efforts to relieve God of the total responsibility for the presence of evil in the world. Advocates of the limited-God view have argued that unless we deny the reality of evil, or postulate a God who is beyond good or evil, or accept the anomaly of a God who somehow reconciles and harmonizes the two, then the concept of a limited God is inescapable.

One must acknowledge that the concept of a limited God is attractive when compared to some traditional doctrines of an infinite God. The limited-God concept takes realistic account of the reality of evil; it echoes the terrible conditions actually existing in the world. Evil is real in human experience; humanity's battle against evil is actual, and it should be recognized. A limited-God view enhances the importance of human beings, making possible a stronger sense of comradeship with God in the common struggle to achieve the right. This sense of participation and responsibility gives one incentive to join the fight, if right is to be up and out. Everyone likes to feel important. The conflict is real and engages our total energies. God needs our human help in the moral struggle. Therefore, human beings must assume their rightful portion of responsibility, if God and right are to win.

An absolutist view of God might fail to attract people to the common human/divine struggle against evil. If God has already predetermined the complete victory of good over evil, one need only quietly wait (Quietism) for God's ultimate triumph. Or, if it works the other way, we might as well wait just as quietly for defeat. If assured victory be not the case, if God is viewed as less than all-powerful, all-knowing, and all-good, we cannot conclude that the battle cannot be won by evil. So, why fight?

But to this defeatist attitude, one must answer morally to the contrary: Unless one fears diminishing God's majesty by denying God's infinity, it is far more degrading to God's divine nature to believe that God could eliminate evil but does not care enough for good to do so. Stated differently: Better a limited God than one who is morally neutral towards pain and the purpose and end of his creation. For Black Theology, even if God be conceived of as weak in his arms, he must not be thought of as weak in the knees. God must be a God of absolute goodness, who wills only the good for his creation. If God be otherwise, some more adequate understanding of evil is needed.

Black Theology, however, has never accepted the notion of a God limited in power, either. Black people have won too few victories. The odds—with a few exceptions—are so much stacked against Black people that they need to adhere to an absolute view of God and his power to win against all external forces of evil. There must be no doubt about his caring or his victory. An oppressed people must have complete assurance of the ultimate victory of the good God. Oppressed people necessarily reject the concept of a weak God, whether in muscle-power or in morals.

Dualism as an Answer to the Theodicy Question

The limited-God concept leads to a dualistic metaphysics, which pictures the world process as a ceaseless struggle between the almost equal forces of good and evil. The ancient Persian religion of Zoroaster personified in Ahura Mazda (the Wise Lord) and Ahriman (the Opponent) the two principals in the contest between darkness and the light. Edwin Lewis[13] of Drew University and Ruth Nanda Anshen[14] are latter-day exponents of cosmic dualism, Lewis exploring it as a vast, all-encompassing, cosmic struggle between God and Satan; Anshen regarding it psychologically. Using an objective devil symbol like John Milton did in *Paradise Lost* and reading the Genesis story in the Bible, Anshen sees each human being as containing within the individual, inner consciousness a cosmic conflict of the dual forces. Each person must choose which side to serve.

The God-Beyond-Good-and-Evil Answer
to the Theodicy Question

According to another view, God is beyond all good and evil conceptualized by humans. God's will and purpose, like the divine being, are infinitely different from human realities, including limited conceptions of good and evil. Hence, there is no logical contradiction in holding that these apparent opposites are reconciled and harmonized in God. God's ways—just like God's standards of evil and good—are not the same as ours. Much that seems evil now may, in fact, be good, but it lies beyond our finite human understanding in God's ultimate purpose. Evil to us may be good in God's mind and purposes. If we could see the whole cosmic process, as God views it, if we could see teleologically to the end of his creative process, much that we now consider evil we could see as good—or, if not good in itself, then at least evil mitigated as a necessary adjunct to the good.

The God-beyond-good-and-evil concept provokes immediate objections. It rings like theological double-talk: Placing God beyond good and evil, one

---

[13]Edwin Lewis, *The Creator and the Adversary* (New York: Abingdon Press, 1948)

[14]Ruth Nanda Anshen, *The Reality of the Devil: Evil in Man* (New York: Harper &Row, 1972).

seems to say that evil is really not evil or that evil is good. At the same time, we must agree with linguistic empiricism, that the significance of any term derived from human experience is something else in the experience of God, whom we cannot even conceive, much less understand. Nevertheless, to say that evil does not exist is not the answer to the problem of evil. Some more reasonable explanation is needed, if Black Theology is to address altogether existential human suffering.

THE THEODICY QUESTION
AND IMPERSONAL CONCEPTS OF GOD

The quest for an understanding of God and evil must not be confused with concepts that do not meet the basic criteria for God. God is no product of a mere "subjective faith-knowledge" (Hegel) or "faith-need" (Feuerbach) or even "religious illusion" (Freud). God is a being who is personal and central to Black religious belief. The strongest doubts in the minds of Black religionists have traditionally been about the goodness and justice of God, not the fact of his existence. Black spirituals, the oral religious tradition, Black literature, the theology of the Black church derived from its preachers, all attest to the divine interest in human affairs, and all accept the reality of the existence of a Divine Being.[15]

Most concepts of God in traditional Black belief relate to God's attributes in proof of how deeply God cares for his creation. The religious orientation of Black people attempts to make sense out of concrete human existence and to explain the presence of evil in the world as it impinges directly on them. This is the approach because the God of the Black religious experience is personal. To understand God and evil more fully, one must look at evil in terms of how it touches God personally. The theodicy question may be most troublesome precisely for those religious thinkers who conceive of God as a personal—and therefore a caring—being. Even a personalist understanding of God and evil is not entirely satisfactory; but partial answers are our lot. By contrasting what impersonalist and atheistic explanations lack with what a Black personalist God-concept offers, one can see why Black people of faith prefer a God who cares—with all the theological problems that entails—to a world of blind forces that do not care.

Atheistic thinkers have no external living God to blame for the existence of evil. If, as with Hegel and his followers, God and man are one; if God is

---

[15]See Benjamin E. Mays, *The Negro's God;* also, Gayraud S. Wilmore, *Black Religion and Black Radicalism,* 1-39; James H. Cone, *The Spirituals and the Blues* (New York: Seabury Press, 1972) 70.

no more than the subjective entity of the human mind; if God is no more than man's lost self-esteem externalized in a subjective concept—then the theodicy question is inapplicable. If, as with Feuerbach and his followers, God is not an independent reality, but the collective identity that humans project to represent their highest possibilities; and if these perfected projections are the objective end of their striving—then the theodicy question again does not apply. Theodicy becomes a troublesome question only for those who hold to an objective authentic "God reality."[16]

Similarly, no room exists for the theodicy question among the "death-of-God" thinkers, because God has "died in our time, in our history, in our existence"; and therefore, "He is not present in the current world of faith."[17] If God is dead, we do not have to explain evil. But "death-of-God" conclusions are uncommon in the Black community of faith. There were no "death-of-God" Black theologians.

Potentially of no greater interest to Black Theologians is the theistic naturalism that has been developed for the most part by Process theologians influenced by the philosophy of Alfred North Whitehead. At most, however, its relevance to Black religious thought is limited.

For Whitehead and other Process thinkers, God is at one with the natural order. God does not transcend the unfolding process; he is a part of it. The problem of how a transcendent God created an imperfect world is sidestepped: Process theology's God merely affirmed to be at one with the natural order, as God did not create the natural processes from the outside. God works from within, under conditions generally conceded to be more favorable for him than for human beings. Process theologians do allow that God is relational for us.

Daniel D. Williams, a leader in early Process thought, perceived love as the central Christian concept. Williams' system of theology relates God to us by use of the love symbol. He conceives of God in dynamic temporal terms— God must respond to what is currently taking place within the world. For Williams, God's love has the capacity to take a variety of forms, nor can we grasp God's love under any single ontological form. Indeed, God's love and wrath are so woven together in the divine character, they have but one meaning. God's love can become "suffering love" to deal with the suffering of the

---

[16]Howard R. Burkle, *The Non-Existence of God* (New York: Herder and Herder, 1969) 90-99.

[17]Thomas J. J. Altizer and William Hamilton, *Radical Theology and the Death of God* (Indianapolis: Bobbs Merrill, 1966) 11, 46ff.

world. Individuality, freedom, action and suffering, causality and impartiality are all means of expressing God as love.[18]

In common with other Process thinkers, both philosophers and theologians, Williams believes that the basic category for understanding reality is "event" rather than "substance." God is thus conceived of as "dynamic process" or "event," not as an existing being. Williams follows his teacher, Henry Nelson Weiman, who described God as "that behavior of the universe . . . which preserves and increases to the maximum the total good of all human life where right adjustment is made."[19] For Williams, as for Weiman, God is the process of progressive integration, the "creative event," and the growth of the "qualitative meaning." These verbal nouns denote be-*ing* as movement and activity, not *be*-ing as ontological substance. Williams contends "that God does suffer as 'He' participates in the on-going life of the society of beings." But in Williams' thought, God's suffering seems to be only impersonal, notwithstanding that "his" sharing the suffering that arises in the world is the supreme instance of knowing, accepting, and transforming it by means of love. In this sense, God is a kind of cosmically divine sensitivity; Without it, to be sure, no sense at all could be derived from the substantial being of God.

Williams did not specifically relate his understanding of God's love to Black human suffering. No consistently Process-oriented theology has been published yet by a Black theologian.[20] Perhaps this is because Williams' approach and that of Process theology is insufficient as a conceptualization of the personal God. Williams' interpretations are often confusing; he never states clearly if God moves only within the process or transcends it. If God "be," his being must surely reflect some transcendent, independent structure needed in a description of divine love. But because Williams' thought had trouble placing the ontological locus of divine structures, one wonders if God, for Williams, is not involved in evil and could be made directly responsible for it. In Process thought, God is certainly qualified by the negative aspect of evil,

---

[18]Daniel Day Williams, *The Spirit and Forms of Love* (New York: Harper & Row, 1969) 121, 210.

[19]John Macquarrie, *Thinking about God* (New York: Harper & Row, 1975) 216ff. Cf. also Daniel D. Williams, "Tradition and Experience in American Theology," *Religion in American Life,* ed. J. S. Smith and A. L. Jamison (Princeton: Princeton University Press, 1961) 466; and *What Present-Day Theologians Are Thinking* (New York: Harper & Row, 1967) 73.

[20]Eulalio R. Balthasar, *The Dark Center* (New York: Paulist Press, 1973) may be an exception. Balthasar would describe himself as a Process thinker; however, his attempt to adapt Process thought to Black Theology is weak. Neither does he adequately address the problem of evil.

namely discord in the absence of harmony. Process thinkers might counter, as Weiman would, to say that although evil is obstructive, it may thereby clash with evil so as to result in a positive end. But this negation of the transcendent nature of God and the identification of God with the creative processes render Process theology unattractive to Black thinkers. Process thought is dressed in the right symbols, but the meanings are alien. Black people have lived too close to evil and suffering in "the process" to accept the impersonal God of Process thought, who, although he suffers lovingly the evil of the process, seems impotent to change the anti-Black process. Process theology offers no clear "God object" to which Blacks may direct baffling questions.

Even fewer Black people would agree with Christian Scientists, who contend that evil is merely a false perception, and that rationally improved and more mature thinking demonstrate that only goodness exists. Optimists, whether religious or nonreligious, typically try to make evil good, or say that evil is a misunderstood concept, or exhort us that good will eventually come even from what we conceive to be evil.

Various other "natural" explanations of evil are available, all of them interesting, none of them satisfying to anyone with a taste for Black theology. Instrumentalists hold that evil is a prod or spur—like running a temperature when you're sick—that helps us keep our eyes on the good. Romantic socialists (Rousseau) see evil as a product of urban circumstances, which have "spoiled rustic goodness and turned the noble savage into an ignoble citizen."[21]

Others—quite apart from the question of God's existence—ignore or deny the reality of evil. They have reduced human malevolence (literally "wishing to do ill") to human ignorance, error, or mental blindness. Malevolence is also seen as the root of characterological sadism, a behavior viewed as the direct result of stress, or as the manifestation of a subhuman, prior instinct of aggression. Other interpretations describe malevolence as "the animal in man," a lag in human development which the evolutionary process has not yet overcome. All these definitions take "evil" as a natural human condition needing to be forgiven, or better understood.[22]

These anthropological constructs, supplemented by metaphysical and religious concepts, often do not accord evil a clear status of reality in human experience. In the absence of a more ontological approach, one senses a tendency to play verbal games with the real and unpleasant realities of evil, a ten-

---

[21]Paul W. Pruyser, *Between Belief and Unbelief* (New York: Harper & Row, 1974) 173.

[22]Ibid., 174-75.

dency that extends to calling evil the mere absence of good, when in reality malevolence is much more than merely the absence of benevolence.

A HUMANOCENTRIC ANSWER
TO THE THEODICY QUESTION

In keeping with nontheistic religious thinkers, William R. Jones believes that the power lying at the heart of all things works towards order and goodness, but this power is limited.[23] According to Jones, this power does not do more because it cannot. He conceives of God as less than a theistic or personal being; however, one must wonder whether William R. Jones has offered God any theological help by allowing God to limit himself. Weak as a theistic God's power may be, the task of erecting a moral order within an indifferent universe is even a bigger problem for an impersonal God. According to William R. Jones, the world may yet be saved, but salvation will come neither by the will and power of an absolute theistic God (traditional theism) nor by human beings alone (religious humanism). How Jones' conclusion might work, however, he does not make clear. Perhaps an impersonal God in partnership with human beings can impose an adequate moral order and erect an adequate structure of humanizing values needed for world-salvation, regardless of nature's indifference; but William R. Jones is a philosopher, not a pragmatist.

Jones identifies himself as a "humanocentric theist,"[24] a theological position often labeled "religious humanism." While Jones attempts to articulate theistic humanism, he does not seem to grasp the full meaning of the term. Even with Jones' new label, the reader still has trouble conceptualizing God as Jones describes him. The following problems occur: According to Jones, one must ask: "Is God an ontological being, living and existing?" Jones suffers the ambiguities of making God dependent on human aspirants, in that he conceives of a human as the "bearer of the spirit." Here one must reply: Does not human life transcend itself? Is this limited God nothing but the product of human subjective aspirations, projected or objectified? If the God of humanocentric theism is at one with collective human aspirations, then the theodicy question becomes irrelevant. An unontological, untranscendent God is not a conscious being, separate and apart. Being at one with the human problem, he can hardly promise its solution.

Is it God's character or collective man's character which is at stake in Jones' thought? How did God get to be a White racist? Is God's segregationist mind-

---

[23]William R. Jones, "Theism and Religious-Chasm Narrows," *Christian Century* (May 1975): 520.

[24]Ibid., and *Is God a White Racist?*, 20ff.

set part of his inner consciousness or is it an external projection of his onto-logical being? If God were a White racist, he would have to be an ontological being, possessing both a subjective and objective self-consciousness or self-knowledge. If God, the White Racist, is merely a projection of the collective American character, which is mostly White and largely racist, William Jones has not told us anything we did not already know. His accusation against God is little more than a sociologically astute but theologically reductionist an-thropomorphism.

Jones admits that he does not see enough evidence in the world to con-vince him that God is not a White racist. But Jones' conclusion that God is partial to White people is a violation both of the divine infinity and William Jones' epistemological humility. This conclusion presupposes that one could know the sum total of God's acts in the ancient past, the sweaty present, and the teleological future. This conclusion presupposes that one could see the be-ginning and the end, that one could know the creative purpose of God's future actions, and that one could read the acts of God clearly enough to separate them from the acts of human beings.

Jones' theistic humanism makes human beings co-sufferers, co-workers, and co-equals with God. The divine mind-set, past, present, and future as-pirations and heavenly success are all at the mercy of human thought and ac-tion. "Man, have pity on God!" William Jones' argument leaves us with the uneasy conclusion that humans and God struggling collectively together are not assured a victory over the evils of this world.

William R. Jones' limited God-concept is not adequate for suffering Black people of faith.[25] Black people need a God who can make the difference, if they are to have faith in God as the subject of their religious quest, liberation, freedom, salvation, and the ultimate salvation of more than just the Black world. God must be worthy of Black worship. Help from God is surely more needed than human assistance, especially from a powerless people. Black theologians dare not conclude upon a God who is less than personal and all-powerful: There must be no doubt about the outcome of the Black struggle for justice. An absolute God must equal the difference between Black power and Black hope. With or without the help of human beings, God is our ab-solute assurance of ultimate success.

---

[25]Jones, *Is God a White Racist?*, 132-44. Also see Major J. Jones, *Black Awareness: A Theology of Hope,* (New York: Abingdon, 1971) 131. 197,131.

CHAPTER SIX

God Was in Jesus Christ Experiencing What It Means to Be Human

THE HISTORY OF CHRISTOLOGY ACCORDING TO THE BLACK PERSPECTIVE

In discussing the God-concept, I have said very little about Jesus Christ. My emphasis has been on God, the creator. The discussion has centered on God, because we must first see God in the fullness of his being in order to see Jesus Christ as the second person in the God-head. This is especially true in view of the many attempts currently to reinterpret Jesus in the light of contemporary religion and life. When we speak of Jesus Christ in these pages, we are not talking about a different God or some person other than the God of our discussion. To conceive of Jesus Christ separately from God would be to miss the meaning and purpose of the divine advent in human history.

In the unity of God's holy absolute personal responsive being, we concluded that God is sufficient unto himself; all things come from God, and nothing could possibly be added. Now, in looking at Jesus Christ, we shall be viewing God in the aspect of his entrance fully and explicitly into the world to reveal himself to us. In Jesus Christ, Black people see God in a new role. Previously, we looked at God as the creator; now we will view God in the roles of Redeemer and Savior. We see God become flesh, and live as a human being in order personally and responsively to experience what it means to be human. God himself, in the truest sense of the word, becomes a redeemer of his creation.

Black people's quest for God cannot be assessed adequately without attending to the fact that they behold God's ultimate purpose for human life as revealed through Jesus Christ. Without Christ, we cannot understand or comprehend fully what is meant by liberation, freedom, and ultimate salvation. Black theologians insist that any interpretation of Jesus Christ in his relation to God and his meaning for human beings in their quest for liberation, freedom, and salvation must answer and relate to the existential conditions of Black people. Jesus Christ is a highly personal matter for Black people.

In the person and work of Jesus Christ, God entered into human history and took upon himself the limitations and difficulties of human existence (John 1: 4; Phil. 2: 6-8). For the Black theologian, whatever is said about God and his relation to human beings must be related to actual human history. The whole message of Jesus was the proclamation of God, his nature, his power, and his purpose for humanity. The center of attraction was not simply Jesus as man, but the revelation of God through and by Jesus. Jesus Christ, both human and divine, was therefore representative both of God's involvement with his people and of his people in their liberation struggle. No other motif suffices. The quest for salvation must be understood as God's involvement with his people in the world, if it is to be relevant for Blacks.

An adequate interpretation of Jesus Christ begins with a clear affirmation of who he was as a historical person. Theology requires, moreover, that an adequate interpretation of Jesus Christ must also include a fully conceptualized Christological statement of how he was related to God. In God only is our salvation: If Jesus is conceived of as being at one with God, then we must know Jesus in his relation to God in order to accept him as our ultimate means of knowing God. At the same time, if we regard Jesus simply as God, then we are corrected by his own emphatic teachings to the contrary that he was not God, as recorded in the Gospels. We must conclude that whether one attempts a Christology in heavenly terms or a Christology in earthly terms, the question of how Jesus Christ was related to God is central to any adequate understanding of them both. Especially for Black Theology, the historical reality of Jesus must be made fruitful and relevant in our minds.

God's presence in Jesus Christ has not always been understood fully as Jesus's unity with God. Understanding of that relationship has undergone a long development. The difficult debates of the ancient church about Jesus' divinity were necessary to grasp the full meaning of God's presence in Jesus Christ and if some rational understanding of Jesus's unity with God was to prevail. In recent times, God's presence in Jesus has been understood in many ways other than the sense of his unity with God. It is necessary to relate the Christological tasks of Black Theology to this conflictual history and development in the theological enterprise.

1. Orthodox Christology articulations have told us that in a single person, Jesus Christ, a completely human nature and a completely divine nature were united. The "very God" and the "very human" natures were completely

united, yet without a reduction of either the humanity or the divinity. The Council of Chalcedon (451) asserted that "our Lord Jesus Christ is to us One and the same Son, the self-same perfect in the Godhead; the self-same perfect in manhood; truly God and truly man; the self-same of a rational soul and body; consubstantial with us according to manhood; like us in all things, sin apart; . . . acknowledge in two natures unconfusedly, unchangeable, indivisible, inseparably; the difference of the natures being in no way removed because of Union."[1]

The Chalcedonian argument for the union of the human and the divine is conceptual language, without absolute or historical proof of the unity of being. The language contends that Jesus Christ was truly God and truly man, that his divinity and humanity were completely distinct and unchanged, and that they were perfectly united without separation in the one personhood.

While we may contend in monotheistic language that God is "One" and not "Two" or "Three," traditional trinitarian theology has left unanswered the related question of what happened to God in the coming of Jesus Christ; nor, heretofore, has Black Theology extended its discussion to include this Christological issue. It is the appropriate theological task of Black theologians to discuss the personal, relational effects on God himself of the full unity of his being with Jesus Christ.

2. The apostle Paul was avoiding the first Christian heresy, that Jesus merely "seemed" to be human when he quoted the hymn in Philippians 2: 5-7 to say that when the eternal God became incarnate, he "emptied himself" of the attributes that essentially distinguish God from man. In the incarnation, God lived on earth without infinite power, absolute knowledge, or space and time transcendence. Influential theologians—among them, Donald M. Baillie and Emil Brunner—have missed this point.[2] But to believe that the Son in dramatic, deceptive pretense stepped out of the Godhead for a while, later to return to unity in God again, is neither orthodox nor more plausible than the methodological theophanies of paganism.

3. The extreme opposite from Docetism contends that Jesus was and is merely a man, howbeit of unusual religious insight into the nature of both God and man. He devoted his great powers to the high purposes of teaching and healing until his unswerving loyalty to duty and his lofty ideals led him

---

[1]T. Herbert Bindley, *The Ecumenical Documents of the Faith*, 4th ed., ed. F. W. Green (London: Methuen and Co., Ltd., 1950) 234-35.

[2]Emil Brunner, *The Mediator*, trans. Olive Wyon (London: Lutterworth Press, 1934); Donald M. Baillie, *God Was in Christ* (New York: Charles Scribner and Sons, 1948) 88-90.

to martyrdom. Jesus was not divine, but the human "religious ultimate"; not the incarnate second person of the Godhead, but—at most—superhuman.[3] John Hick and other post-enlightenment theologians downgrade the concept of incarnation, calling it myth.[4] The view of Jesus as an "enhanced human" has become popular. Black Theology must address the growth of this rationalist view in the Black community of faith.

4. Rudolph Bultmann separated the Christ of faith from the historical Jesus. His school of thought contends that our historical sources of information are so fragmented and biased that we are left uncertain about the Jesus of history. For Bultmannians, establishing the historical person is difficulty enough; confessing Jesus to be the incarnate second Person of the Godhead is purest existential faith-commitment. Bultmann preached that we should follow Paul, fix upon the Christ of faith, and not worry about knowing the unknowable Jesus of history. The meaning of Jesus is futuristic to the existentialist believer, and therefore Jesus' history—except for the Cross—is not necessary for people of faith. Bultmann reasoned that

> . . . neither in the earliest Church nor anywhere in the New Testament is Jesus looked back upon as a deed of God by which—as by Abraham, Moses or David—He showed "mercy" upon the people. Of course not! For Jesus' importance as Messiah—Son-of-man—lies not at all in what he did in the past, but entirely in what is expected of him for the future.[5]

There seems, however, to have been sufficient proof of the historical Jesus—in New Testament history, his remembered teachings, records of his exceptional deeds, expressions of faith in the early church, and the comments of those who knew him in the flesh—enough to know that his life cannot be doubted. The Jesus of history ought never to be taken lightly. Without him there is no adequate example of what human life ought be. Those who knew him then—just as those who know him now—were legion.

5. William Hamilton—a "death-of-God" theologian—replaces faith in God with a substituted devotion ("faith-embrace") of the Jesus of history. To be a Christian is to render loving service to humanity in Jesus' name. For Hamilton, Jesus is well-enough known via the New Testament to provide a

---

[3]Donald T. Rowlingson, *Jesus, the Religious Ultimate* (New York: Macmillan Company, 1961).

[4]See John Hick, ed., *The Myth of God Incarnate* (Philadelphia: Westminster Press, 1977).

[5]Rudolf Bultmann, *Theology of the New Testament,* trans. Kendrick Grobel (New York: Charles Scribner's Sons, 1951) 36, 293-94.

positive focus for the Christian's faith and life. Thus, the Christian is "bound to Jesus by obedience to him; as obedient to him as he was obedient to God." Hamilton emphasizes Jesus almost to the total neglect of God: "Jesus is the one to whom I repair, the one before whom I stand, the one whose way with others is also to be my way, because there is something there, in his words, his life, his way with others, his death, that I do not find elsewhere. I am drawn to him, and I have given him my allegiance."[6] Hamilton articulates a one-dimensional faith in Jesus, a this-worldly religious stance that moves the person of faith to a life for others, lived in radical obedience to the Jesus of history whom Hamilton has selected. This Jesus replaces the God who died in a kind of incarnate Christological atheism. Immanentism to the core, Hamilton's faith and theology proceed without a traditional, transcendent God, thereby excusing Hamilton, almost, from consideration of the God-Jesus relationship.

6. Thomas J. J. Altizer—another "death-of-God" theologian—answers the Christological question under the influence of Nietzsche, Hegel, William Blake, and Mircea Eliade. Citing Paul's doctrine of kenosis (Phil. 2: 7-8), Altizer contends that the death-of-God denotes the self-annihilation or total self-negation of God. By sacrificing itself, God's "being" becomes "its own other"; and in so doing, "being" becomes the opposite of its own original identity.[7] This process is representative of "God emptying himself" or incarnating himself in Christ. God died to become at one with Jesus Christ in order to embody himself redemptively in the world.[8] God, the transcendent source and ground of all existence, totally emptied himself of sovereignty and transcendence to become the man in Jesus Christ. God did this to make possible his final reconciliation with the world; his initial self-negation in Christ continues to be actualized throughout the total range of human experience. Through this unintelligible descent into concrete human history of all the fullness of God's being, primordial God has emptied himself of his original life and power and now steadily recedes into some kind of alien other, an unconceptual lifeless nothing.[9] Death-of-God Christologies are totally alien to any current Black religious experience.

---

[6]William Hamilton, "The Shape of a Radical Theology," in *Radical Theology and the Death of God,* ed. Thomas J. J. Altizer and William Hamilton (Indianapolis: Bobbs-Merrill, 1966) 171.

[7]Thomas J. J. Altizer, *The Gospel of Christian Atheism* (Philadelphia: Westminster Press, 1966) 106ff. and 71.

[8]See also S. Paul Schilling's views on Altizer in *God in an Age of Atheism* (New York: Abingdon, 1969) ch. 2.

[9]Altizer, *The Gospel of Christian Atheism,* 108.

7. A seventh view of the God-Christ relation is sometimes called the Progressive Incarnation theory. Instead of God emptying himself in a divine condescension or self-negation, the incarnation is understood to be an ethical process presupposing intimate interaction between the man and the Logos. In this way, it identifies within all humans a direct kinship to God, a spiritual receptivity that makes possible a developmental incarnation upward from the human to the divine. This ethical process was a gradual, developmental growth within the consciousness of Jesus Christ, to whom the Logos communicated itself to such a degree that Jesus gradually and actively became God. Though not the same, the Progressive Incarnation theory is akin to Wolfhart Pannenberg's view.[10]

8. The father of Liberal Protestant theology, F. D. E. Schleiermacher and, to a degree, Albrecht Ritschl shared an understanding of the God-Jesus relationship that one might call Jesus' "God-consciousness."[11] Rejecting the two-nature theory of orthodoxy, they contended that Jesus' divinity did not contain a metaphysical or ontological at-oneness with God. Jesus' unity with God was a spiritual or mental state, a God-consciousness that was itself a divine indwelling. In the tradition stemming from Schleiermacher, nothing further of a divine nature or essence is needed to make God real as a resident of indwelling consciousness and identify God's proper habitat as human experience. A high quality of God-consciousness is presumed possible in all human beings, just as it occurred in Jesus, so long as one opens the "self" to God-consciousness.

A Black theologian would, I suggest, typically judge this assortment of White Christologies, as sketched above, to be a retreat from the Christological richness of Christianity in general and the Black religious experience in particular. Without engaging each of the above-mentioned Christologians specifically in debate, we must maintain on behalf of Black Theology our emphasis on the responsive personal holy nature of God's being, and not back off from that emphasis when we come to say, moreover, that God was in Christ Jesus. In Black Theology, we neither separate Jesus and God and see them as apart, nor do we empty God out or subject him to Jesus Christ. Of course, there is the occasional exception to the Black Christological norm. The proper introduction to an understanding of Black Theology's view of God's presence in Christ as Creator, Redeemer, and continuing Presence in the Holy Spirit is, I contend, an accurate historical understanding

---

[10]Wolfhart Pannenberg, *Jesus, God and Man* (Philadelphia: Westminster Press, 1973).

[11]F. D. E. Schleiermacher, *The Christian Faith* (Edinburgh, Scotland: T. & T. Clark, 1928) 402.

of the early Christian experience. The people who knew Jesus personally and experienced the holy response to their human need in a man who behaved like God were the first to know what others later also knew—what we have known in the Black religious experience. Black Christians and early Christians have at least this in common: Both communities looked up from the troubles and oppression of this world to behold an actual revelation of God in who Jesus was and what he did. That was their experience; the words to describe the experience came next.

The Revelation of God in the Person and Work of Jesus Christ

The early Christians did not start out with a theological formula that God was "three-in-one." The concept of the trinity arose historically and developmentally out of the revelatory experiences of the early church. They had met Jesus personally and had experienced in him the person, the presence, and the holiness of God's very own being. Having had those experiences, they had to ask themselves how best to conceive of God, now that they had met Jesus Christ.

Since most of the earliest Christians were Jews, they naturally drew on the Old Testament Scriptures for their God-concept. In the Old Testament, God—for Isaiah—was a God of sovereign power. For Jeremiah, God's call was to personal piety. For Ezekiel, God was a great and holy person. For Amos, he was a God of justice. For Hosea, he was a God of love. Taken together, each of these aspects contributed to a developmental view of the primary attributes of God inherited from Judaism by Christianity.

The trinity concept of God began when the early Christians faced the need to explain Jesus Christ, whom they knew and thought to be divine. They had known him in both his fullness and freshness of being. Through him, they were developing a broader sense of God's being. Those who knew Jesus Christ sensed through him that the Father God of the Incarnate Word was wonderfully new, distinct, and a person not fully known or conceptualized before. They were seeing what God was like in the person and work of Jesus Christ. Yet they could also see in Jesus Christ, but with a new clearness, the God of old. The Hebrew "Shema" belonged also to the Christians: "Hear, O Israel: The Lord our God, the Lord is One" (Deut. 6: 5 and Mk. 12: 29). In the unity of these two, the God of old and the God now revealed in Christ as Incarnate Word, early Christians were compelled by their experience to find a way to describe Jesus Christ in his relation to God and to explain the relation of God to Jesus Christ.

One of the ways they found to express this relationship—though by no means the only way—was the trinity-concept, as summarized in a trinitarian formula rare in the New Testament: Matthew 28:19. In the "Great Commission," the disciples are charged by the Risen Lord to "Go, therefore, and make disciples of all nations, baptizing them in the name of the Father and of the Son and of the

Holy Spirit." This verse has been questioned in terms of its textual support in the most ancient manuscripts, and there is little to indicate whether the "three" were each and all understood to be God—"three and yet one," to say nothing of the theoretical language about persons, modes, substances, hypostases, procession and the other high-theological diction that emerged in subsequent centuries. Nevertheless, Matthew 28:19 (and other passages) stand at the head of a long line of constant development, suggestive of a trinitarian God-concept—however undeveloped, as yet—among the early Christians.

In the unity of God's holy personal being, we must always be clear, revelation is not the work of three separate beings, however closely united. In every particular, revelation is always of God in the full oneness of his being. The trinity-concept says that God has revealed himself to us from the unity of his personhood in three different ways. In the Trinity, the unity of God himself is, indeed, unimpaired; so that, when we distinguish among the Revealer, the Revealed, and the Revealed-ness of God, we affirm, nevertheless, a Unified One. God is one yet the fullness of his being expresses three modes of existence. Therefore, God the Father, God the Son, and God the Holy Spirit are to be understood in terms of their mutual relationships.

Revelation, we may therefore conclude, is not the work of three persons, however closely united; it is the work of God in his oneness of being. God has revealed himself to us from the unity of his personhood in three different ways. This point of view can be called "modalism" and works as an African-Hebraic corrective to the tendency towards tritheism implicit in Greek and Latin Christian theology. Karl Barth also saw the need for this correction: "We begin the doctrine of revelation with the Triune God. . . . God, himself, is unimpaired unity; yet, also, in unimpaired difference is Revealer, Revealed and Revealedness. . . . We prefer to say the three 'modes of being in God,' rather than three persons. [This means] . . . that He is not in one mode only, but rather he is . . . in the mode of the Father, in the mode of the Son, and in the mode of the Holy Spirit."[12]

God himself, not the trinitarian God-concept or any other particular theory about the divine nature, is the central focus of the Black church. God is One and God is triune—these are theological givens, taken for granted in Black Theology. The modalistic correction of orthodox formulas has found a curious but informative summary in the name of a particular Black denomination—"The Church of God in Christ." But Black Theology has spent little energy debating "how" the personal and holy God made his presence known in Jesus

---

[12]Karl Barth, *The Doctrine of the Word of God,* trans. G. T. Thomson (Edinburgh, Scotland: T. & T. Clark, 1936) 1: 1: 339, 400-404.

Christ. Rather, Black theological talk is about our faith that God was doing something in Christ for our redemption. Again, a rich assortment of related terms is taken for granted in the Black church: the life, death, and resurrection of Jesus; the offices of Jesus as prophet, priest, and king; and much more. But, as with our understanding of God, the person and work of Christ as the redeemer is taken most seriously when we consider Jesus Christ not only as the savior of souls but also as the liberator of his people. We are chiefly interested in Christology in this narrower sense: What is God attempting to achieve for Black people through Jesus Christ?

When we assess the above mentioned aspects of Jesus' life or the three offices traditionally ascribed to him, one sees immediately the imperative of addressing the Christological power of these traditonal concepts to the unique experiences of the Black Christian community. For example, the work of Christ in terms of three offices is said to culminate in the production of a vital religious experience. Christ's royal dignity manifests itself in our struggle to triumph over the world. His prophetic revelation brings us a God of religious assurance. His priestly mediatorship reestablishes our sin-disturbed communion with a loving God who has identified with the humanness of humanity. When living faith in and knowledge of God is awakened within persons, then Christ fulfills his threefold office as God revealed. But there is a weakness in this threefold scheme: Nothing here necessarily establishes a felt-connection between the work of Christ and the experiences of the believer. We must elaborate the pattern of that connection between God and us through Jesus Christ.

For the Black Christian, the great love of a personal responsive holy God for human beings becomes real only to the degree that by the power of such a love, God overcomes human beings and incites them to corresponding love. This way, the people secure forgiveness of their sins. Through his passion, Christ becomes important to the Black Christian because he reconciles human beings to God and wins from God for the people immunity from punishment and guilt, a guilt derived from our not having been what we were meant to be. With these two achievements—love and release—Jesus Christ delivers human beings from the powers of this evil world and opens the door to a new life.

With this more or less classic representation of the traditional doctrine of the atonement, we combine Anselm's concern for divine satisfaction and Abelard's concern for the power of love to influence for the good. Within these commonplaces of Christian thought, we can see God at work reconciling human beings to one another and reconciling the world to himself. The potential for healing broken relationships latent in these holy concepts far excels ordinary ability to describe human mutuality and forgiveness. Social scientists, indeed, seem much more astute in describing how we humans fall into disruptive conflicts, hatred, and alienation than they do in explaining how we are to pick ourselves up again.

But still, nothing has yet been said to make clear the relevance of these sacred terms in particular for Black people. Jesus Christ was about God's business of forgiveness in the broadest sense; and our Christological task must not be defined so as to narrow our interest away from a subject less wide than all creation itself. Therefore, we reformulate every Christological question across the full range of God's own experience in Jesus Christ as he lived among us, when we ask: "What does this mean for Black people?"

JESUS CHRIST IN AFRO-AMERICAN PERSPECTIVE

Jesus Christ in the Black religious experience is neither merely a Christological concept nor the subject of extensive theological debate. He is, rather, a living reality, fully identified with the sufferings of Black people because of his own sufferings in this world.

Black people have occasionally argued about Jesus, however. Opinion polarized over the question of Jesus's color during the discussion of the concept of the Black Messiah. Sometimes the question becomes overheated on how closely Jesus' experiences paralleled the experiences of his Black followers. The nature of these two points of debate indicate that Black Theology must relate Jesus to the total experience and aspirations of Black people. Like other groups who have re-created Jesus after their own image, Black Christians are interested in Jesus Christ to the extent that through him they can experience the liberating power of God for them. Deotis Roberts expresses it this way: "An oppressed people can behold the human face of God only through the Jesus who, as a man, lived the very life of God."[13] Roberts argues that a role for Jesus Christ can be established in the Afro-American Black community of faith best by rejecting the narrowed Jesus who is a captive of Euro-American culture. Christ is above culture, says Roberts, and at the same time at work in culture and history towards redemptive ends.[14] Only a universal Christ could be adequate, Roberts insists, one who would be equally existentially meaningful to all races, Blacks included, a Christ to confront humanity in all historical and cultural situations. Speaking for Black Theology, he contends that: "If we give our Christology the right shape, we may be helpful in making Christ the 'Desire of all nations.' In one sense, however, Christ must be said to be universal and, therefore, 'colorless.' "[15]

---

[13]J. Deotis Roberts, *A Black Political Theology* (Philadelphia: Westminster Press, 1974) 116.

[14]Ibid., 119.

[15]J. Deotis Roberts, *Liberation and Reconciliation: A Black Theology* (Philadelphia: Westminster Press, 1971) 139.

In sharp contrast to Roberts' universalizing view, James H. Cone argues for
a particularized Black Christology. Cone takes the view, exceptional to the Black
theological norm, that the Black church is Christocentric and that Black Theology does not distinguish Jesus from God. Cone collapses the distinction of the
human and divine natures in the person of the risen and struggling Savior.

> We do not have to choose between a Christology either "from below" or "from
> above." Instead, we should keep both in dialectical relation, recognizing that
> Christ's meaning for us today is found in our encounter with the historical
> Jesus, as the Crucified and Risen Lord who is present with us in the struggle
> for freedom. Indeed, it is Jesus's soteriological value as revealed in his past,
> experienced in our present, and promised in God's future that makes us know
> that it is worthwhile indeed, necessary, to inquire about his person.[16]

Albert Cleage, inspired by Marcus Garvey's Black Utopianism and informed by S. G. F. Brandon's study, *Jesus and the Zealots,* insisted that Jesus
Christ was a Black Messiah. Apart from what color Jesus' skin was, Cleage
was essentially right to stress Jesus' identification with the oppressed poor of
his homeland. Jesus gave aid and direction to their struggle for freedom; he
made whole the dignity of personhood.[17]

In Jesus Christ, God had entered the battle for human wholeness. In Jesus
Christ, God had exerted his power to redeem, emancipate, and liberate a people
oppressed. In Jesus, the oppressed dare to hope more than their oppressors dare
to see. Whether Jews in the Roman Empire or Blacks in White America, any
oppressed people can find God's most decisive act of liberation for them in the
life and ministry of Jesus Christ. This is why Albert Cleage asserted that "the
theological need for the Gospel of liberation can be found in the life and teachings
of Jesus; not in His death, but in His life . . . God reconciled men unto Himself
in the life and teachings of Jesus which gave men a new conception of human
dignity and inspired them to fight to be men instead of slaves."[18]

In Cleage's thought, one encounters a radically different Jesus than is
common in the Black community of faith. Cleage insists that Jesus was phys-
ically black and a messianic member of the Zealot Party mentioned in the New
Testament. Cleage's Jesus was not a "gentle Jesus, meek and mild." Rather
Jesus was the Black Messiah and a leading revolutionary of his time.

In contrast, Cone and Roberts make of Jesus a symbolic Black Messiah,
without implication for his genetic code. Even though Cone and Roberts avoid

---

[16]James H. Cone, *God of the Oppressed* (New York: Seabury Press, 1975) 121.

[17]Albert B. Cleage, *The Black Messiah* (New York: Sheed and Ward, 1968).

[18]Albert B. Cleage, Jr., *Black Christian Nationalism: New Directions for the Black
Church* (New York: William Morrow and Co., 1972) 188.

the literal sense of Cleage's historically unfounded hypothesis, their symbolic use of the term "Black Messiah" is key to their understanding of who Jesus was, is, and will be in contemporary Black Theology. Roberts has suggested that many Black people now look to a "political Jesus" rather than to a Jesus "at one" with any given culture, be it Black or Euro-American. This direct identification of Jesus with the Black struggle sets Black Christology apart from the abstract and theologically convoluted White expressions of Christology arrayed above. As J. Deotis Roberts proclaims, "Jesus spoke to the needs of Black people to be whole persons in a society in which they are 'mere faces in the crowd.' " Jesus speaks to Black people's need for peoplehood. Jesus brings hope and assurance to a people "seeking some place to be home."[19] Most Black theologians, in fact, stop short of Cleage's literalism; they do not, however, fall short of his meaning. Black Theology believes in Jesus in all the generic senses of traditional Christology; but more importantly, Black theologians consistently revise the meaning of Jesus as specifically pertinent to Black people, as specifically the Christ of their liberation. Consider, for three more examples, the thought of Joseph A. Johnson, Howard Thurman, and Olin P. Moyd, along with a fourth, especially in the poetry of Countee Cullen.

Speaking of the universal importance of Jesus for Black people, Bishop Joseph A. Johnson, in a paper which he gave at Andover Newton Theological Seminary shortly before his untimely death, asserted that "the people of all races, because of his service, are able to identify with him and to see in his humanity a reflection of their own images. Today the Black man looks at Jesus—observes his ministry of love and liberation and considers him the Black Messiah who fights oppression and sets the captive free."[20]

The universality that Johnson saw in Jesus' service of loving liberation Howard Thurman attributes to the appearance of the spirit of Jesus among the oppressed:

> The basic fact is that Christianity, as it was born in the mind of this Jewish teacher and thinker, appears as a technique of survival for the oppressed. That it becomes, through the intervening years, a religion of the powerful and dominant, used sometimes as an instrument of oppression, must not tempt us into believing that it was, thus, in the mind and life of Jesus. . . . Whenever his spirit appears, the oppressed gathers fresh courage; for He announced

---

[19]Roberts, *A Black Political Theology*, 117ff.

[20]Joseph A. Johnson, unpublished paper given at the Autumn 1969 Convention, Andover Newton Theological Seminary.

good news that fear, hypocrisy and hatred—the three hounds of hell that track the trail of the disinherited—need have no dominion over them.[21]

Olin P. Moyd addresses the ubiquity in time and place of Jesus among the downtrodden and ascribes an emergent quality to Christology that springs immediately out of the people's response to Jesus who is liberating them.

> It is through what Jesus has done and is now doing in the Black community that Black people have come to understand who He is. And, thus, any Christology emerging out of the Black religious experience is essentially emerging out of the Black response to the redemptive events of Jesus as He is known in Black history. . . . Jesus was, is, and always will be the Redeemer of the disinherited.[22]

Everywhere among the oppressed, his spirit appearing among the disinherited to redeem and liberate them, Jesus is "real" for Black people because what he does for them is "real." They look to him for an eternal inheritance, to be sure; that is a Christological given of traditional theology. But they put particular stress on the social, political, and this-worldly spiritual liberation that Jesus is effecting among them now. On this account, Moyd reasons that the balanced reception of Jesus as the Savior from sin and guilt and the Liberator from oppression recommends Black Theology as offering a balanced Christology. "This is what Black theology is all about. In Black religious thought, both dimensions . . . the Jesus of history and the Christ of faith . . . have always had their rightful place as per the Black religious expression."[23]

This difference in Black Theology's Christological emphasis contrasts sharply with the highly abstract Christologies of White theologians. Typically, the Christologies of White Euro-American theologians have been either bloodless or bloody: either remote from the actual social, economic, and political needs of people and therefore remote from Jesus the liberator, or the creature of the oppressor and the implement of oppression and therefore remote from Jesus the liberator. The cause of this drastic difference between Black Christology and White is that Black Christologians arise from an oppressed community, whereas White ones usually do not. I agree with Moyd's analysis:

> Like the quest for the historical Jesus, the quest for a Black Theology—a theology of redemption—is a struggle against tyranny of the overriding Euro-

---

[21]Howard Thurman, *Jesus and the Disinherited* (New York: Abingdon Press, 1949) 29.

[22]Olin P. Moyd, *Redemption in Black Theology* (Valley Forge PA: Judson Press, 1974) 140, 142.

[23]Ibid., 142.

American creeds, doctrines, and the theologies. These creeds, doctrines and theologies have been formulated by the oppressor class, by the wealthy, and by the socially and politically powerful rulers of the Western world. Consciously, or unconsciously, they were also formulated for the oppressors and the power brokers of the West. There was no need for an interpretation which would promote the idea of Jesus as Redeemer from human-caused oppressions. Through military, economic and political might, they were their own redeemers from threatening nations. This is particularly true of America. This was the position, philosophy and the theology emerging out of Germany. It is the culture and ideals of the ruling class which shape the attitudes and acts of a nation. And it is the culture of the nation which shapes the theology of those who participate in the benefits derived from national policies.[24]

White theologians, because they were not members of an oppressed community like the Black community, have had the leisure to indulge in this lack of Christological balance, opting now for the "Jesus of history," now for the "Christ of faith." They have been out of touch with the Black community, except for the occasional sit-in and a sentimental attraction to Black folks' religion, and therefore remained out of touch with Black Theology and uninfluenced by Black Christology, which, until recently, have been mostly oral traditions and therefore available only to White or Black Christologians who were willing to be in touch with the living voice of the Black experience.

Had White theologians paid attention to Black Christology, they might have been able to rectify this lack of balance by achieving a liberation Christology—a living Christology that balances the needs of both the oppressors and the oppressed and that goes beyond mere balance to new Christological creations. As Moyd says, Black Christology is not a mere writing of another life of Christ; it is, rather, a liberating reflection upon and interpretation of the Black religious experience. It aims to lead the believer to encounter the risen Redeemer who is the Liberator of both the oppressor and the oppressed. Black Christology fuses the "Jesus of history" together with the "Christ of faith" into a third, new man—the Black Messiah of liberation.

Because Jesus Christ is existentially at one with the deepest dimensions of the most brutal experiences of the Black community of faith suffering at the hands of the oppressor, the best resource for evaluating Black Christology is the poetic literature that has risen from the Black community's deep need for identification with the divine. This is the emphasis in the poetry of Countee Cullen, who wrote "The Black Christ" in 1929.[25] His poem is a moving in-

---

[24]Ibid.

[25]Countee Cullen, *On These I Stand* (1930; rpt., New York: Harper & Row, 1947) 126—an anthology of Cullen's earlier works.

terpretation of how God, in Jesus Christ, identifies with Black suffering in the excruciating experiences of the then frequent lynchings of Black people.

Countee Cullen, son of the pastor of the Salem Methodist Episcopal Church in New York City, had a deep sense of theology but a deeper sense of God-forsakenness. Cullen's thought moved analogically between the similarities he perceived in the experiences of Black people in bondage and the sufferings of Christ. The cry of Christ from the cross became for the Black poet the cry of Black people being lynched. This pattern of analogical fusion of two realities experientially expressed had been characteristic of Black symbolism, as seen in the juxtaposition of the work of the deliverer Moses and the work of the deliverer Jesus.[26] Perhaps the first to associate Black lynchings with the crucifixion in a published work, Cullen's poetic view of the atonement retained its poignance right through the revolutionary days of the Civil Rights Movement and beyond. Speaking for all Black people searching for identity, dignity and assurance of the presence of God, Cullen expressed anxiety over the question of the color of God in another poem, "Heritage." In "The Black Christ," although Cullen confessed that he belonged to "Jesus of the twice-turned cheek," nevertheless he still could not make his "precedent of pain" Black like himself. In deep despair, Cullen yearned in agony for a God who is real and related to Black suffering; in hesitant language, he groped towards a Jesus who could be at one with the Black condition:

> . . . My conversion came high-priced;
> I belong to Jesus Christ, . . .
> Lamb of God, although I speak
> With my mouth thus, in my heart
> Do I play a double part . . .
> Wishing he I served were black. . . .

As though asking forgiveness for this musing, but with a renewed boldness, Cullen asserts:

> . . . Lord, I fashion Gods, too;
> Daring to give You
> Dark despairing features where,
> Crowned with dark rebellious hair,
> Patience wavers just so much as

---

[26]Eugene D. Genovese, *Roll, Jordan, Roll: The World the Slaves Made* (New York: Random House, 1976) 245-55.

> Mortal grief compels, while touches
> Quick and hot, of anger rise
> To smitten cheek and weary eyes.
> Lord, forgive me if my need
> Sometimes shapes a human creed.[27]

The South, the poet cried, was "crucifying Christ again and again" in its lynchings of Black people. He condemned the lynchings in his "Christ Recrucified."

> . . . Christ's awful wrong was that He's dark of hue
> The sin for which no blamelessness atones;
> But lest the sameness of the cross would tire,
> They kill him now with famished tongues of fire;
> And while he burns, good men, and women, too,
> Shout, battling for his Black and brittle bones. . . .[28]

In the battle waged between his pagan-self and his Christian-self, between belief and unbelief, Cullen attempted to find some rational understanding of the fate of Black people at the hands of the White oppressors—even pious Christians. In "The Black Christ," Cullen attempted to deal with questions of faith compelled by his confrontation with a pro-White culture that willed the death of a people. "He sings about a Black boy, Jim, growing to manhood, proud and handsome, about his temptation to reject the faith in the face of injustice, about his crucifixion for the sake of love, and murder, and about his resurrection appearance. He sings about Jim's brother, who acknowledges Jesus as well as Jim of the same kin."[29]

Cullen did not dissolve his painful awareness of the brutality of the crucifixions of his time into abstract doctrines of the atonement. He wanted his readers to experience the first Calvary and God's sacrificial love by equating lynching with the crucifixion, Jesus with Jim. This is Jim speaking:

> God knows I would be kind, let live, speak fair,
> Require an honest debt with more than just.
> And love for Christ's dear sake, these shapes that
> Wear a pride that has its genesis in dust;

---

[27]Cullen, "The Black Christ" in *On These I Stand*, 27-28.

[28]Ibid.

[29]Ibid., 106.

The meek are promised much in a book I know
But one grows weary turning cheek to blow.[30]

Cullen's Christology is best expressed in the first lines of "The Black Christ," in which he struck the first chord that put the lynchings of Black people in harmony with Christ's crucifixion.

How Calvary in Palestine
Extended down to me and mine,
Who but the first leaf in line
Of trees on which a man should swing
World without end, in suffering
For all men's healing, let me sing.[31]

Cullen did not interpret Christ's crucifixion in terms of sacrifice to satisfy the wounded honor of God or as paying the debt for human sins. Rather, he interpreted it as the work of God who is with us and for us in the agony of oppression. He sees in Jesus the God who is with Black people, God exploring human pain at its most human level. In "The Black Christ," while Jim is not the Savior, but rather one whose death points back to Christ, Christ is the continual evidence that God is forever at one with the human condition symbolized in Jim. God dignifies our suffering lives even at the limits of the most arbitrary kinds of human oppression by being at one with human beings. This is the Black doctrine of the "at-one-ment."

Another poet of the Harlem Renaissance, Langston Hughes, totally rejected the suffering Christ and would have him gone. In 1933 Hughes wrote "A New Song" about Christ.

The day is past
I know full well now
Jesus could not die for me—
That only my own hands
Dark as the earth
Can make my earth-dark body free.[32]

---

[30]Ibid., 85.

[31]Ibid., 27.

[32]Cited in Benjamin E. Mays, *The Negro's God* (New York: Atheneum, 1973), 238-39.

Indeed, Hughes rejected the Christ of liberation for the ways of this world. In doing so, he added to the literature of bitterness, struggling on without a God who would be with human beings in all conditions.

For Black people, Jesus Christ, in his person, life, and work, brought God into clear focus as at one with the human condition. In the oral and written traditions of the Black community of faith, especially in poems, the spirituals, and the sermons, one hears the evidence that in birth, life, and death, Jesus Christ cast his lot with the oppressed people: the suffering, the needy, the sinful, and the disinherited. In the Black religious experience, Jesus is a personal and claimed experience of God himself who is with us. The Black Messiah suffers on the cross of our lynchings and rises out of our suffering to liberate us from our suffering.

AN AFRO-AMERICAN INTERPRETATION
OF GOD'S HUMAN EXPERIENCE IN JESUS CHRIST

To assert that God himself is capable of human experience is not to reduce the divine nature any more than to say that God himself suffered is Patripassionism. To identify God with Jesus Christ is not the same as equating the Father with Jesus. Neither is it to suggest that God was at one personally with Jesus Christ but with no one else. Rather, it is to say that something took place radically, in the very root of the personhood of God, when God expressed himself in the person and work of Jesus Christ. Indeed, how could God have taken flesh from the womb of a lowly Maiden, making it his own, and still remained the same? How could God have undergone a birth like ours, the divine coming forth a human being, and still remained the same? Nevertheless, when we say that he truly became a human person by the assumption of human mind and soul, flesh and blood, we also believe that God still remained truly God in nature and person. To say that God remained God, however, is not to say that God did not change.

In a moving passage, James Cone contends that to understand the Incarnation is to know Jesus in relation to our blackness and in relation to what we have suffered for no reason other than our color.

> The convergence of Jesus Christ and the Black experience is the meaning of the Incarnation. Because God became man in Jesus Christ, he disclosed the divine will to be with humanity in our wretchedness. And because we Blacks accept his presence in Jesus as the true definition of our humanity, blackness and divinity are dialectically bound together as one reality. This is the theological meaning of the paradoxical assertion about the primacy of the Black experience and Jesus Christ as witnessed in the Scriptures.[33]

---

[33]Cone, *God of the Oppressed*, 36.

In Cone's Christology, primacy is given to blackness and to Scriptural sources, rather than to the theological and philosophical speculations characteristic of Euro-American thinkers. Cone is aware of the White theological tradition, but his emphasis is different because he writes out of the Black religious experience. "The importance of Scripture as the witness to Jesus Christ does not mean that Black Theology can, therefore, ignore the tradition and history of Western Christianity. It only means that our study of that tradition must be done in the light of the Word disclosed in Scripture as interpreted by Black people."[34]

For the Black community of faith, the results of any adequate Black Christological formulations must present Jesus Christ in the light of Black religious experience. No conclusions will suffice that do not describe who Jesus was, what he did, and what he said as the direct expression and implementation of God in action, doing "divine things humanly," among Black people and on their behalf. We are concerned here with whether it can be said of Jesus' life, teachings, and death that God was experiencing in Jesus Christ what it was like to be human the same way we Black humans have experienced that condition. When God sees us and meets us and judges us, are we being seen, met, and judged by a God who has actually experienced and now knows, at the lowest human level, what it means to be human? The Christ event must disclose the initiative, the involvement of God who is "very God of very God" and "very human of very human," in the Black experience of life and death, if Christology is to make any claims on Black allegiance. But, when one believes that God was experiencing in Christ what it is like to be human, then a new question about God himself has to be answered: How did God's experience of the human condition in Christ Jesus change God himself? And the second question to be answered is like the first: How did God's experience of the human condition in Christ Jesus change humanity? Did God himself become a different God as a result of this experience? Did the human condition change?

Jürgen Moltmann, the "theologian of hope," is the European theologian who, among White theologians, has contributed the most to Third-World theologies and Liberation Theology around the world. Although Moltmann did not himself arise from an oppressed people and although his theological style is the sophisticated method of the German university, his imagination, nevertheless, has allowed him to conceive that something happened to God in the Christ event, especially on the cross.[35] Because Moltmann has grasped this all-important point, one may make a beginning of comparing him with

[34]Ibid., 31.

[35]Jürgen Moltmann, *The Crucified God* (New York: Harper & Row, 1974).

another Liberation theologian, James H. Cone. Cone, for quite another set of reasons and more directly, also understands the effects upon God in his commitment to the Christ experience: Because Jesus was at one with the poor and the oppressed, and God and Jesus were at one with each other, God is at one with the poor and the oppressed.[36] God is not merely static and non-responsive, the Mover unmoved by what happens to his creatures. For both Moltmann and Cone, God cares.

This is not to suggest that God is capricious, subject to external change, or relates to his creation by whimsical moods. Nevertheless, the eternal being of the God who was revealed most clearly in Jesus Christ was touched through that divine human encounter. In the New Testament, we read that whom humans seek in their finitude and transitoriness, became human in Jesus Christ. "He is the image of the invisible God" (Col. 1: 15). Black people have traditionally insisted on this fully human characterization of God, which is, at the same time, a fully divine characterization of Jesus. In Black Theology, we sang about the mystery of the incarnation: "God Knows Just How Much We Can Bear." How, one may ask, do Black people come to this sophisticated theological conclusion so untheologically?

The mystery of Jesus Christ is revealed in the incarnation of God, the incarnation of an eternal, original, unchangeable being brought into this sphere of temporal, decaying, transitory existence, where we humans live and must die. Because in Jesus Christ the eternal presence of God among human beings is encountered, the salvation of the world is found in him. Quoting Moltmann: "God became human so that human beings could, by experience, partake of God. He took on transitory, mortal being, for that which is transitory and mortal to become intransitory and immortal."[37] In God's act of becoming human, something happened to him and something also happened to his creation.

The apostle Paul instructs us that the death of Jesus on the cross must be understood as God's action, even as God's suffering. He explains what "God in Christ was doing." God not only acted in the crucifixion of Jesus by sorrowfully allowing it to take place, but God himself took active part with his own being in the dying Jesus. God, as incarnate Word, was acutely at one with Jesus Christ, suffering with him (2 Cor. 5: 19-21). This is Paul's paradox of the God-man. How can the almighty God be at one with a helpless man? Both Cone[38] and Moltmann[39] follow Paul to identify God in Jesus Christ

---

[36]Cone, *God of the Oppressed*.

[37]Moltmann, *The Crucified God*, 88.

[38]Cone, *God of the Oppressed*, 108ff.

[39]Moltmann, *The Crucified God*, 214, 222.

with human suffering, thereby committing God to suffering in the person of Jesus. Moltmann makes the point both more cogent and more paradoxical when he asks: "How can God, himself, be in one who has been forsaken by God?"

Black suffering looks without blinking at the coming of Christ in order to understand itself. Christ was sent by God and sent to suffer so that we would no longer be slaves but could be liberated so as to become heirs (Gal. 4: 3-7). If God, who sends another to suffer, cannot himself suffer, then he cannot care. Black Theology maintains its unique identity among world theologies with its emphasis on God's suffering care.

Black Theology upholds that within the inner-personal unity of the trinity of divine beings (God *ad intra*), the responsive relationship in holiness of the Father with the Son and the Holy Spirit was not subject to changes wrought upon God by external events. This does not, however, preclude God's freedom and ability to determine upon self-change. The content of God's consciousness is not so fixed that it cannot—if God will it—be constantly changing to include future events, as yet unknown in their non-being. We believe human actions to be truly free, such that whereas God's knowledge of the past is total and absolute, God's knowledge of future events is not yet complete, particularly so far as acts of human freedom are concerned. The perfection of divine omniscience, then, must be construed to be God's always perfectly increasing knowledge taking in, with the passage of time, all knowable reality as it expands. Not to know as real and sure what is, as yet, neither sure nor real, is not imperfection; to know the unreal and the unsure as uncertain and still forming is to know perfectly whatever is to be known. God could, of course, preclude uncertainty by determining beforehand what is to be and what all are to become; the high price he would pay for this, however, would be the freedom of his creatures to develop and grow.[40]

Moltmann astutely modifies the usual notion of God's unchangeableness by appealing to the Nicene Creed, in its anathema against Arius. That God is unchangeable, says Moltmann, is not an absolute statement:

> . . . it is only a simile. God is not changeable as creatures are changeable. However, the conclusion should not be drawn from this that God is unchangeable in every respect, for this negative definition merely says that God is under no constraint from that which is not God. The negation of changeableness by which a general distinction is drawn between God and man must not lead to the conclusion that he is intrinsically unchangeable. If God is not passively changeable by other external things like creatures, this does not mean

---

[40]See L. Harold DeWolf, *A Theology of the Living Church* (New York: Harper & Brothers, 1953) 102.

that he is not free to change himself, or even free to allow himself to be changed
by others of his own free will. True, God cannot be divided like his creation,
but he can still communicate himself.[41]

Following Moltmann's line of thought, we conclude that God is capable
of experience; that the Word incarnate in Jesus Christ was actually God revealed, or God himself communicated. God's Word communicated in human
flesh was not, of course, the total inner being of God's holy personal triune
self. The Father and the Holy Spirit are not the Word. God and the Word are
not the same, but they must be taken together (with the Holy Spirit), as a
unity, if they are to explain God in the fullness of his being. God is at one
with his Word, because his "Word" is communication of his being.

Because God in Christ was experiencing what it means to be human,
moreover, we further conclude that before God's communication as a human
being, God had not fully experienced human suffering. God had known about
human suffering, but he had not suffered. Being "other than human," God
could not himself involve with reality as a human without becoming a human
being. Suffering and injustice had not affected him personally before he experienced injustice and suffering in Christ. Prior to his coming to earth in Jesus Christ, God's total otherness meant that he could not be affected by any
of the actual experiences of the human condition. God could not weep, having
no tears. Citing Moltmann again,

> . . . one who cannot suffer cannot fully love either. A God who is only om-
> nipotent is in himself an incomplete being, for he cannot experience help-
> lessness and powerlessness. . . . What sort of being, then, would be a God
> who was only "almighty"? He would be a being without experience, a being
> without destiny, and a being who is loved by no one.[42]

Black Theology agrees with Moltmann in this. Who better than Black
people know that we become truly human in community with the incarnate,
the suffering, the loving, the human God in his communicated Word, the
flesh and the person and word of Jesus Christ? This truest expression of God's
love is made outwardly permanent and everlasting only in the humanity of
God. This divine experience *ad extra* illuminates the life of God *ad intra* and
makes clear the inner movement of the three divine persons in mutual suffering and joy, love and pain, the giving and taking of God's own personal and
reciprocal life. In relation to Jesus Christ, God has experienced changeable-
ness, thereby perfecting his knowledge.

---

[41]Moltmann, *The Crucified God*, 229.

[42]Ibid., 222.

Theological legend has it that when the second person of the Godhead, having become human, returned to heaven to re-enfold himself into the Father's bosom, God himself was different. God had voluntarily opened himself to being affected by others, to experience what it is like to be fully human. Now God knew as only one can know who has become vulnerable, poor, and oppressed—a self other than a God-self. Now God had experienced the acceptance and rejection of others motivated not by their attitude toward God but by their attitude towards a fellow human being. God, as communicated Word, had assumed humanity, possibility and passibility of sharing human suffering. For the first time, God achieved a new freedom: the freedom to know suffering from within, as a result of the "otherness" of the "other." This was the experience that changed God's very nature. God in Christ for the first time could know another's disappointment; know another's hate and feel another's rejection; know what it means to be abandoned; know what it means even to die on a cross. By exposing his love at the deepest level of human risk, God became fully acquainted with the human condition for the first time. Thereby the Godhead acquired a new dimension. God had taken human being into his bosom and his very being. Moltmann, who significantly titled his book *The Crucified God,* explains the mystery of the Trinity of suffering this way:

> The Son suffers dying, the Father suffers the death of the Son. The grief of the Father here is just as important as the death of the Son. The fatherlessness of the Son is matched by the sonlessness of the Father, and if God has constituted himself as the Father of Jesus Christ, then, he also suffers the death of his Fatherhood in the death of the Son.[43]

In Black Theology, we seek to make God's relation to Jesus more personal and particular. Black Christology particularizes God's redemptive act and relates it to the struggle of Black people. The human depth of the "Word was made flesh" in Jesus Christ that Black people clearly see is self-identification with an oppressed people's struggles and aspirations. This same God relates through Jesus Christ to Black people in their situation. Jesus Christ was a divine epiphany in the midst of his people; as a divine presence, Jesus Christ continues to be God's identification with his people, fulfilling his ancient promise to be with them, even from prior times in ancestral Africa.

Gayraud S. Wilmore got it right when he said: "Jesus Christ is crucial to Black Christianity because darkness was his experience, and we know something about darkness. The Good Friday spiritual asks the question, "Were you there?" And the unspoken answer is, "Yes, we were all there when the

---

[43]Ibid., 243.

'Nigger of Galilee' was lynched in Jerusalem." Is there any wonder that we can identify with him."[44]

And James Cone got it right when he said that unless God, in Jesus Christ, can understand what "blackness means, then he cannot know what it has meant historically to be Black. Indeed, the importance of the identification is to have God actually experience it by being Black. If Black people thought Jesus did not know what it means to be Black, they would not be Christian. In him, God becomes the oppressed one and thus reveals that the achievement of full humanity is consistent with his being."[45]

Moltmann theologizes about "the crucified God" and Cone theologizes about the God who became Black. Wilmore identifies Jesus as the "lynched Nigger of Galilee" and Countee Cullen could understand Jesus because he was Black and he had seen Black people being lynched. These theologians are all talking about the God Black people sing about, when they ask: "Were you there?" And when they sing: "He knows just how much one can bear," they are telling what Black Theology knows about what the Black God learned in the darkest of all human experiences. They are singing their faith in God, who in Jesus Christ experienced what it means to be human, even to be a Black human being.

In this close identification of Jesus with a people's suffering, most Black theologians reject the idea of redemptive suffering. Suffering is not praised, but, rather, relativized as a "sign to an arrogant, self-aggrandizing, rebellious generation,"[46] more burdensome example than a redemptive requirement. Beginning with Black thinkers in the years of slavery, through Martin Luther King, Jr., down to contemporary Black theologians with but few exceptions, we reject any identification of oppression and suffering with redemption. Blackness for Black Theology is not what it was said to be by generations of White theologians—a sign of God's wrath. Blackness is not a sign of punishment for being Black; it is rather a profound and mysterious assignment from God by which Black people have been called to bear witness to the message of his judgment and his grace to all nations, and especially to White America.[47] Like Jesus the outcast, preaching his Outcast Theology as he started his earthly ministry, Black Theology takes as its own the Liberator's mission "

---

[44]Gayraud S. Wilmore, "Blackness as Sign and Assignment," in *Black Preaching: Select Sermons in the Presbyterian Tradition*, ed. Robert T. Newbold, Jr. (Philadelphia: Geneva Press, 1977) 165ff.

[45]Cone, *A Black Theology of Liberation*, 20.

[46]Ibid., 173.

[47]Ibid., 172-73.

. . . to bind up the wounds of the afflicted and to liberate those who are in prison, and to set free those who are oppressed."[48]

God's Blackness does not negate his Whiteness or his Brownness. In African myth, the divine is sometimes referred to as the chameleon. God has taken on oppression in all the colors of human skin. Neither does one have to be Black to be able to grasp Black Theology. Abraham Heschel—neither Black nor trinitarian nor Christian—spoke for an oppressed people when he described this going out of God as the "situation of God" in what Heschel calls "pathos theology." God, says the Jewish theologian, is quite different from the capricious, envious, and heroic divinities of the mythical sagas, subject to fate and external change. The Lord God is affected by human beings because he is supremely interested in every facet of his creation. The pathos of God— God's suffering—is intentional and transitive. God relates outside himself to the history of his people. For Heschel, God has already emerged outside himself in the world at the creation; therafter, the history of God cannot be separated from the history of his people. God is not at one with his creation or history, but neither can he be separated from history or his creatures. This means that God's history is that both of oppressed peoples and of oppressor peoples, though the histories are different. God knows each people at the level of historical experience and relates to people in the differentness of their individual and collective histories.[49]

When Black theologians speak of the final and complete self-humiliation of God in his identification with Black people in the person of Jesus Christ, they are saying that God in the person of Jesus enters into the finite situation of each human's individual and collective life in history. In doing so, God accepts every condition of humanness and embraces the whole of human existence within his own being. God did not become an angelic spirit, so that human beings would first have to soar to the realms of the divine in order to participate in God. God became a human, so that he can participate in humanity, and humanity in him. Neither did he restrict partnership to an elected people, so that they only by their obedience to a covenant might enter into his fellowship. Rather, God lowered himself and freely accepted the worst conditions of the human race, bar none. He came incarnate in a person, subject to all human limitations and to all inhuman treatments, so that each person, however limited or inhumanely treated, may participate in him with the wholeness of life.

---

[48]Ibid., 204.

[49]Abraham Heschel, *The Prophets* (New York: Harper & Row, 1962) and *God in Search of Man* (New York: Octagon Press, 1976) 157ff.

By allowing himself to become human, even to become Black, by experiencing the death of his Son as communicated Word, the innermost life of God the Father himself was changed forever. In the subsequent reunion with the very-God/very-man life of Jesus Christ, God himself realized a new dimension of love for the godless. In his return to Godhead, the Jesus Christ of history, as the second person in the Godhead, brought from his human experience a new fullness of being to the inner life of God. God who became Black in his communicated Word-made-flesh in Jesus Christ now knows the full scope of the human situation from the inside. God himself became a different God, for now he knows just how much human beings can bear.

CHAPTER SEVEN

Eventuating in the Holy Spirit: God's Continuing Personal Responsive Being with Us Still

THE MEANING OF THE HOLY SPIRIT GAINED THROUGH HUMAN HISTORY

We have thus far defined God as a holy responsive personal being. We have described Jesus Christ as the communicated incarnate word of God. We have looked at the relation between God and Jesus Christ as the first and second persons in the Godhead. Then we considered the ontological changes in God's personhood that resulted from his experiencing humanity in his self-communicated incarnate Word. Now we want to ask how the Holy Spirit is related to God and to Jesus Christ in the oneness of God's Being. As before, we are stating a Black Theology—inquiring how the Holy Spirit relates to the Black human condition.

Because God is a trinity of holy responsive personal beings, one cannot fully conceptualize God and Jesus Christ without understanding the Holy Spirit. In the same way that we pursued a God-concept in terms of what makes sense to Black people about being human, Black Theology proceeds to develop its own view of the Holy Spirit.[1]

Beginning with a distinction in correction of a popular misconception, Black Theology's view of the Holy Spirit is not to be equated with that of the

---

[1] Henry H. Mitchell, *Black Belief* (New York: Harper & Row, 1975) 136-52, treats the Holy Spirit more in keeping with Baptist-Church theology than in a consistently Black-theological personalist, relational way.

charismatic and Pentecostal movements of the twentieth century, although Black believers appreciate the value of these current religious movements. The understanding of the Holy Spirit in the more narrow tradition of Afro-American religion has its historical roots in more explicitly trinitarian and traditional Christian thought.

In traditional Christian thought, the Holy Spirit is acknowledged as the third person of the Godhead. In a broader sense, the Holy Spirit is a testimony to the many-sided nature of God. We may assign every aspect of the divine being and activity that can not be readily accounted for in terms of God as Father and Creator or of Jesus Christ as Son and Liberator to the work and role of the Holy Spirit. The Holy Spirit has kept the Christian's thoughts of God open to new discoveries springing forth from the new and never-ending relations of God. The Spirit of God is God-at-hand, and, in another sense, God-at-work.[2]

In the Christian's striving for perfection, the action of the Holy Spirit is to seal and direct one's ascent to God, bringing us into conformity with divine goals. One of the main ways that the Holy Spirit has directly related to Black people has been in terms of keeping them aimed in God's direction in the quest for liberation, freedom, and salvation. The other main way the Holy Spirit has sanctified Black people is through an abiding, personal and relational presence. God and Jesus Christ, fused, returned to us in the person of the Holy Spirit; now, in the unity of divine personhood, the Father and the Son abide among us in the person and the work of the Holy Spirit. Throughout the long ordeals of slavery and oppression, the nearness of God among Black people was a needed dimension of the slave's faith. Without a sense of God's nearness, the slaves could not have survived the suffering.

Because Black people have been personally familiar in their relationship to the Holy Spirit, they have been at home with the concept of the Holy Spirit as existing in relation to God as a reponsive personal being. As the Holy Spirit, the third person of the Godhead, has always been a personal being, the Holy Spirit has always made God known to Black persons of faith as part of their human experience. The Holy Spirit's role in the Black human existence has been the central work of God in personal relation to the human race, namely maintaining and renewing our needed unity of being. Similarly, as the Holy Spirit is the continuing agent in God's plan for human identity, growth, and development, so also does the Holy Spirit relate to the continuity of the saving work of God in Jesus Christ. God's communicated Word in Jesus Christ was

---

[2]Henry P. Van Dusen, *Spirit, Son and Father* (New York: Charles Scribner's Sons, 1958) 18ff.

objective and is subjective. Objectively, it was an event of God's penetrating into history; after that, it is an ongoing event of God's revelatory actions to human beings. The Holy Spirit is the subject of God's continuing revelations. As we perceive God, we apprehend the divine presence and activity within our lives; this apprehension of God within us, in our subjective inner being, is a grace of God's work within us through the Holy Spirit. Without the Holy Spirit, all of our personal claims on God would be only to an objective God outside us, totally external, utterly holy in a wholly otherness. With the Holy Spirit, we can make a subjective claim for God as the sustainer of our own innermost reality.

The Third Person, the Holy Spirit, is that divine subjectivity in God who relates and is personally akin to the Father and the Son, just as the subjective core of a human being sustains inner life. Through the person of the invisible, indwelling, subjective Holy Spirit, God becomes a subjective living reality within the lives of human beings—spirit meeting spirit. The Holy Spirit is that subjective reality who relates God personally to the inner core of human existence. In the person of the Holy Spirit, God is present and active with and within us, a God-awareness continuously present in every moment of human history (Matt. 28: 20; John 14: 16).

Combining these two chief aspects of the Spirit's work—being God's nearness and aiming us at God's goal of perfection—Martin Luther King, Jr. connected Holy Subjectivity with the human subjectivity of Black people, as follows:

> Let us realize that as we struggle for justice and freedom, we have cosmic companionship. . . . The God that we worship . . . is an ever living God who forever works through history for the establishment of his kingdom. . . . The cross is the eternal expression of the length to which God will go in order to restore broken community. The resurrection is a symbol of God's triumph over all the forces that seek to block community. The Holy Spirit is the continuing of created reality that moves through history.[3]

The Holy Spirit awakens in human beings the realization of our deepest possible kinship with God, an awakening brought about by God the Spirit, already immanent in human beings. The Holy Spirit is God's means of inspiring an awareness of divine availability to any individual who is willing to open up to God's presence and perfecting. Relating the work of the Holy Spirit specifically to Black people, James Cone reminds us that they have believed that "the Spirit is God's guarantee that the little ones are never—no, not ever—left alone in their struggle for freedom. It is God's way of being with people

---

[3]From King's "Prayer Pilgrimage for Freedom" address, 17 May 1957, 4.

and enabling them to shout for joy, even when they have no empirical evidence in their lives to warrant happiness.[4]

This sense of God within, assuring us that "We are God's" and "He is ours," has kept Black people's faith-knowledge alive throughout their captivity, enslavement, and oppression. Indigenous awareness of the Spirit's presence has been the Holy Spirit's own work within the life and history of the Afro-American Black people. The faith-knowledge imparted by the Holy Spirit by means of the Black religious experience has been three-dimensional and twofold: It is a dual knowledge about God and ourselves in relation to God; and, it is a knowledge of the relational, three-person life of Holy God. The Spirit brings to faith a knowledge of himself; the Spirit brings a broader, deeper, second knowledge of the communicated Word of God in Jesus Christ; and the Spirit refreshes the prior knowledge of our God who was first known from ancient times. In the three modes of God's being, we can see God in the fullness of ultimate unitary being. The ongoing work of the Holy Spirit makes available to us the infinite resources of God. The Holy Spirit's offer of continuing ever-fresh revelation of God's truth has been received by Black people as holy empowering to lead us into the fullness of the larger truth we needed to see us through the struggles toward full freedom and equal human dignity.

The inner working of God through the Holy Spirit has accomplished within us a parallel three-dimensional gift of grace: fullness of knowledge of God, forgiveness in Jesus Christ, and freedom in the Holy Spirit.

1. Black Theology, as discussed above, upholds both the objective otherness of God as the creator and ground of all existence and the supreme personality of God as a responsive personal being divinely interested in human beings. This caring Creator goes out to human beings not only at the beginning when God said "Let there be," but also forever, making known his current presence among and within human beings as Holy Spirit. In the Holy Spirit, the totality of God's whole creative being is available to humans, whom he invites to respond to him as a personal God in reciprocal personal awareness. God's grace resides in the movement of the Holy Spirit toward human beings. In the person of the Holy Spirit, grace is that spontaneity in God's nature through which he comes to his creatures to renew, inform, and transform their existence.

2. The forgiveness of God effected through Jesus Christ results in our full confidence that God has accepted each one of us, whoever we are and in spite of what our wrongdoings have been. In Jesus Christ, God approached us, creating

---

[4]James H. Cone, "Sanctification and Liberation in the Black Religious Tradition," in *Sanctification and Liberation,* ed. Theodore Runyan (New York: Abingdon Press, 1981) 178.

a climate of forgiveness. He did not deepen the wounds of guilt by rejecting the human approach in which we seek forgiveness; rather, he made it possible for us to confess our guilt in the knowledge that he would say: "Neither do I condemn you." This degree of confidence can be ours only because we know that God has already approached us the offenders, in forgiveness and love. God's forgiveness is the premise of our full freedom. Human beings must be free to respond to or to reject God's gift of forgiveness. Because the Son makes us free, we are free indeed; and where the Spirit of the Lord is, there is freedom.

3. The freest response to God, by definition, comes from the deepest recesses of human subjectivity; and it is the Holy Spirit who plumbs those depths with the liberating grace of God. It is the Spirit who creates the conditions in an individual's life and, liberated by grace, they can shake off unfreedom. Unfreedom is that godless condition of seeking one's own freedom without regard for another's freedom—without giving or receiving grace. Freedom, then, becomes possible only as a response to another's true act of forgiveness: Because God has forgiven us so much, we can forgive the little or lot that others owe us. God understands us utterly, because of his experience of being human in the person of Jesus Christ; now, fused with Jesus Christ, God returns to us in the person of the Holy Spirit, who is the constant updating of God's understanding of the human condition.

Streaming freely towards us in the prevenient grace of the Holy Spirit, God heads off our unfreedom in every way. He is God ever before us, God ever behind us, and God ever within human beings. In a redemptive sense, the Holy Spirit just never lets a person be, but is forever tracking us down, refusing to leave us alone snug in our unfreedom, content with the lot of a well-kept slave. Redemption in the Holy Spirit is liberation to decision-making (either for or against God, either for or against the fellow-freedoms of our brother and sister humans) and redemption for perfection—the never-ending process of becoming.

It was this Holy Spirit of freedom and setting free that empowered even slaves to feel strong in a condition wherein otherwise they would have felt weak and helpless. Never negating our personal responsibility or erasing the difficulties of a world of oppression, the Holy Spirit in Black life was the personal proof that God was "God with" his Black people. What we say of the Holy Spirit and the life and history of Black people one can also say of all humans, of each individual and each people in their own terms and their respective conditions.

As we proceed to estimate the value of the Holy Spirit for the Black religious experience, we do so fully aware of the historic neglect paid to the Holy Spirit in traditional Christian theology. We see the Black concept of the Holy Spirit—rich in terms of its African roots and the spiritually experiential nature of Black Afro-American religious expression—as a corrective to this history of neglect.

For some, the Holy Spirit, in spite of being the third person of the God-head, has remained an undeveloped, abstract concept without ontological concreteness of being or personhood. Very often, the Holy Spirit is thought of as little more than the "power" or "movement" of God. For some, the Holy Spirit has been identified almost exclusively with the subjective experiences of the inner person; and it therefore became the catchall for whatever was felt to be the individual personal relationship going on between someone and God or between someone and Jesus—a subjective, inner, personal experience "bet-ter felt than told." For some, the Holy Spirit has been eclipsed by Jesus Christ. In traditionally Christocentric Christianity, God is explained in terms of Jesus Christ: God had made himself perfectly clear in the Word made flesh; there-fore, once you had explained Jesus to your satisfaction, little or nothing more needed to be said about God. And, since the incarnate person of the com-municated Word was and continues to be so clear an historical image, the Holy Spirit, by comparison, has remained fuzzy.

Others, however, know that to speak of God as Father and Son leaves more yet to be said. There is a nearer side of God fully known only in the person and work of the Holy Spirit. This is the side of God that relates God most directly and most intimately with the inner being of each individual human; that keeps God face to face with his creation, and that makes of God's self-revelation in history an ongoing process rather than a onetime shot. Aware-ness of this nearest possible side of God is the deeps of God confronting the deeps of human subjectivity—the only virtue strong enough to keep people from exploiting their own feelings, and yet the divine virtue that makes us God-like. Because we "have spirit" in a way similar to the way "God is Spirit," we possess within ourselves the possibility of becoming, by degrees, more and more like God. Spirit belongs to God, both his own, of course, and ours, for he gave it to us. God's Spirit, therefore, associates us with the highest and is the highest within us.

A student of mine, who helped me by reading this manuscript, raised the question, why the work of the Holy Spirit was described in so many ways. In the following discussion, no "one way" is sought to define the "role" of the Holy Spirit, because the roles of the Spirit are many. The Holy Spirit is in-finite God who was relating to each oppressed spirit in just the way that poor soul needed, to make him or her whole and free and holy. A one-line account of the work of the Holy Spirit within the dark Afro-American religious ex-perience is hardly possible.

THE BLACK CONCEPT OF THE HOLY SPIRIT IN ITS AFRICAN RELIGIOUS ROOTS AND IN THE FLOWERING OF THE BLACK SLAVES' RELIGION

Central to the Christian faith is the belief that God is with us now in the Holy Spirit. Holy Spirit, however, in some form, is a feature of religious belief and experience common to all faiths.[5] As African religious roots are the background of the Afro-American Black religious experience, the Holy Spirit in the slaves' expression of the Christian religion was an updating of a facet of the African religious heritage.

A concept of the "Spirit of God" was a more highly developed theological commonplace among African religions than was any corresponding "divine Son" concept. This was so for many reasons. Africans are chiefly monotheistic and therefore lacking the tendency to imagine that God has a special son or daughter other than all his earthly children. The proper dwelling of God on earth, therefore, is each individual human's subjective inner being—a theological construct that contributes greatly to a sense of personal dignity.

The slave found little in the White Christian religion that recognized his or her personal dignity; even when the slaves became Christians, they edited the religion of their White masters so as not to adopt anything that demeaned their personhood.

Black people did more than fix on Jesus as their Savior beyond this world. As discussed above, Jesus Christ was understood in the Black community to be the Liberator—spiritual, political, and, if necessary, revolutionary. But it was in the tension between faith in Jesus as the Liberator here and faith in Jesus as the Liberator here hereafter that the Holy Spirit did powerful work among Black people. Even though he had been crucified, Jesus had never been totally subjected to the powers of this world; now, in the power of the Holy Spirit, neither need the Black slave be. Jesus Christ was King of kings and Lord of lords; and it was God through Jesus Christ who would eventually set things right for Black people. In the meantime, Blacks kept in personal touch with God through the Holy Spirit and at a distance from the White-folks' world, in which the Black person knew better than to trust. The slave could sing, "Ride on, King Jesus," knowing that Jesus Christ was more powerful than any contrary force at work to negate the slave's personhood. When society and slavery, struggle and poverty all said it wasn't so, the Black person listened instead to the Holy Spirit, who told the truth that comes from God: Black people are people, and they are a people of God. Black Spirituals are filled with references to the Spirit of God.[6]

Even when the slaves stopped to brood, even to question the goodness of God, the Holy Spirit sustained them and gave them an unconquerable hope, forbidding them to fail, upholding them until they should succeed. One Black Spiritual on the work of the Holy Spirit sings it this way:

---

[5]Van Dusen, *Spirit, Son and Father*, 25.

[6]See John Lovell, Jr., *Black Song* (New York: Macmillan 1972) chs. 6 and 20.

Sometimes I get discouraged
And think my work in vain;
But, then, the Holy Spirit revives my soul again.

The song goes on to say, as the music and beat pick up with lively expectation, that "Every time I feel the spirit/ Moving in my heart, I will pray!" This is the experiential reality to which James Cone was pointing in the passage cited above, when he described the "Holy Spirit's presence with the people [as] a liberating experience," one which gave them "another definition of their humanity . . . every Sunday morning."[7]

The Black worshiper knew the visitation of the Holy Spirit within the worship service to bring a new sense of being. Black worship "produces a radical transformation in the people's identity," Cone continues, " . . . the last becomes first, making a radical change in the perception of the self and one's calling in society." In this experience aside, Sunday alone made all the difference in the world to Black Christians. Worship gave strength to the weak, courage to the faint, purpose and hope to those who struggled. In worship, Cone says, "Every person becomes 'somebody.' This new identity announced itself in the way people stood and talked and walked. They carried themselves with the rhythm and bearing of dignity, reassured in their new being that they knew where they were going and what they believed.[8]

With the help and presence of the Holy Spirit, the oppressed people in Black slavery kept fresh and full the knowledge of the presence of God in Jesus Christ, the Liberator. With that assurance, they translated the New Testament concept of the return of Jesus Christ into the return of God and Jesus Christ fused in the Holy spirit. This translation of the God-concept in early Christianity was the reappropriation by Black people to their own use of the sacred presence of God within. In the Holy Spirit, they found God binding themselves to himself in an inseparable oneness of being that nothing could divide.

This concept of the Holy Spirit in the Black religious experience is radically neo-African, but quite different from the spiritualism of witchcraft or voodoo, another neo-African religion in the Americas. Whereas those lesser religions fostered one's power over other human beings and the gods, the Black experience of the Holy Spirit made the slave aware of an inner core of being that was beyond all human conquest, made a person one with God, and gave one power for oneself. Without the unitive being of the Holy Spirit to authenticate Black people's sense of being equally human, they could have been

---

[7]Cone, "Sanctification and Liberation," 176-77.
[8]Ibid., 177.

conquered by the many alien forces counter to them. Because Black people associated the Holy Spirit with the truth of their inner being, the Holy Spirit guided them into truth that was more than intellectual comprehension. The Holy Spirit made alive the slaves' sense of being human, of being equal, of being a person, and the deeper feeling of being interrelated with one another and at one with God. The Holy Spirit brought an unhiddenness of divine existence by laying bare God's being within the deep core of Black human selfhood. Once a person had found this inner core of selfhood, that individual experienced all else through it and was prepared to give his or her all for it. This human response in selfhood to God makes clear, as nothing else can, the liberating work of the Holy Spirit. The Holy Spirit of God freed the slave to live redemptively for other slaves, who were weaker, worse abused, more heavy-laden, and humiliated. Within the invisible Black Church of the slave period, and during the subsequent times of oppression after the Civil War, Black people had an abiding sense that God was with them, in a big way; because of this faith-knowledge, they were assured that, within history and in the future beyond history, they would somehow understand even the "why" of slavery. By giving them this assurance, the indwelling Holy Spirit sustained a "faith-hope" in Black people, a trust in the future creativity of God that upheld them even when the surrounding culture was at its most anti-Black, most oppressive, and most dehumanizing. The Spirit of worship and the demanding God are one in Gayraud S. Wilmore's observation:

> The God who demanded their devotion and the spirit that infused their secret meetings and possessed their souls and bodies in the ecstasy of worship, was not the God of the slave-master, with his whip and gun, nor the God of the plantation preacher, with his segregated services and unctuous injunctions to humility and obedience.[9]

The gospel of the Black Church was from God, who had sent the Liberator in his communicated Word. The worship of the Black church was also from God, who had sent his Holy Spirit, an indwelling teacher and personal agent direct from God to a people in deep distress. This was the flowering in the slaves' religion of African roots deep in the remembered God, now cultivated to fresh growth by Christianity. The fruit of that root and growth and flowering would be harvested in the very lives of Black people.

THE HOLY SPIRIT: PRESERVER OF BLACK PERSONHOOD

The experience of God in all people, I suppose, is greater than human conceptualization and language is able to bear. Black Christians have experienced

---

[9]Gayraud S. Wilmore, *Black Religion and Black Radicalism* (Garden City NY: Doubleday, 1972) 14.

the Holy Spirit more fully than Black theologians have adequately reflected, and the Holy Spirit is still an undernourished theme in Black Theology—which is also the case among White theologians. Black theologians, who have written perceptively about the meaning of God and Jesus Christ in the Black religious experience, have almost entirely neglected the roles of the Holy Spirit in the struggle of Black people for liberation, freedom, and identity. This deficiency in Black Theology makes it weak. Black theologians such as James H. Cone, J. Deotis Roberts, Gayraud S. Wilmore, and others have not enriched their theologies by paying due respect to the Holy Spirit. In his *God of the Oppressed,* James H. Cone follows the Christocentrism of traditional White Protestantism when he suggests that "Jesus Christ is the subject of Black Theology."[10] Perhaps even more so for Black Theology than for White, ignorance of the Holy Spirit is a massive theological failure. After the crucifixion and the return of Jesus Christ to the Father, did not both God the Father and Jesus Christ the Word return to dwell in our midst in the person of the Holy Spirit? To know God fully can mean no less than to know God in the fullness of God's personhood as it is revealed to us now and from now on in the Holy Spirit. But the correction of this systematic theological deficiency for Black people is more than academic; it is existential. The meaning of the Holy Spirit is the meaning of God in the life of the Black people.

Gayraud S. Wilmore implies more than he actually said when he observed that: "The missionary could not, in good conscience, deprecate the presence and mysterious work of the Holy Spirit in the life of the believer."[11] White missionary religion offered to Blacks was not void of the Holy Spirit. This rudimentary introduction to the Holy spirit had far-reaching implications quite out of proportion to the intentions of the White preachers. The Holy Spirit assured a measure of both freedom and continuity with the past; but, unpredictably, the Holy Spirit, as teacher and guide, diverted certain biblical and theological conceptions of Christianity into new structures of belief and practice that served the practical needs of the slaves and their children. Those needs concerned the individual's day-to-day physical and psychic survival; but ultimately, the Holy Spirit was concerned with more than individual survival: The Holy Spirit became the instigator of the slaves' struggle for liberation and freedom, for equality and rights, for economic and political survival—in short, for the total survival of a whole people.

The Holy Spirit, who had been promised as the Paraclete to first-century Christians in a churchly context, came to Black people as a Comforter of the

---

[10]James H. Cone, *God of the Oppressed* (New York: Seabury Press, 1975) 32.

[11]Wilmore, *Black Religion and Black Radicalism,* 33-34.

oppressed, a counselor of liberation, and an Advocate of emancipation. The personal agent of God resident in the world, who had been sent to Christians in the first century as another mediator and alter-ego of Christ, came to Black people in oppression not as the spirits of voodoo come to its practitioners—with blood and horror, fear and the magic of power—but as an inner and interpersonal presence of the holy personal relational God. From his unitary being, life takes its life; and in his healing presence, an inordinately difficult life began to make some sense. "All the truth," into which the risen Christ said the Paraclete would lead his disciples, came to Black people as a truth especially for them. To those with ears to hear, the Spirit was saying: "The White lie about Black people is not God's truth. God's truth is that Black people are his dear children, a positive goodness now, and on their way to something much better." Perhaps more than anything else, the Holy Spirit gave the slaves and their children an assertive faith-knowledge and an unshakable faith-hope that kept them looking to a better day coming. For all these reasons, Black Theology dare not leave an understanding of the long struggle under slavery and post-slavery periods unrelated to the Holy Spirit. In those evil days, when all the external forces were telling Black people, "You are subhuman," "You are nothing," "You cannot be or become this or that," the Holy Spirit—that personal, inner-core kinship with God—was enabling Black people to act and feel, not like slaves or subhuman beings, but like the children of God that we are.

The preservation of Black personhood by the Holy Spirit was a divine act of creation, like the day God said "Let there be," and there was; or like the other day, God the Word said, "Lazarus, come forth!" The spirit of the Black people in holy relationship with the Spirit of God was recreated and came forth a new creation—a theological happening and revelatory event that equals any of God's other mighty acts through history. The Holy Spirit related us in holy wholeness to ourselves, to Jesus Christ, and to God himself.

The Holy Spirit is that subjective sense of the divine, in some way the same in the core of the inner unity of Being itself that the human spirit is in the core of human being. A person's spirit is more than mere ego—the "I" or the "irreducible me." A person's spirit is a fusion of characteristics that makes for the unity of personhood. It is that which keeps one attuned to a meaningful sense of direct communication with one's many selves and with the persons of God. When a person lays hold on this sense of deepened humanity, it is impossible for any external forces to shake it. It is that inner core of being that cannot be crushed or conquered; it supports and is supported by the person's natural resolution to continue to be and to become. The Holy Spirit, residing within the people's selfhood like God in the Temple, became their personhood. From within the selfhood of the person, the personhood of a people was preserved and sustained by God. How else could we explain how Black people made it?

The Holy Spirit, therefore, is God and Christ returned, fused into an eternal oneness, bringing the oppressed people an inward sense of identity to enlighten and strengthen them. The Holy Spirit's role is now, as it was then, to be another communication of God's personal being. God's presence, by definition, is always personal, a fullness of Ultimate Being that is creative and recreative of human being. Unless we receive God as a communicating God, he would remain self-contained and self-sufficient, a frozen deity, an unopened package on the shelf. But God communicates himself, he goes out to his creation; and because he does, we are the fortunate ones, able to receive him in Jesus Christ as God's Logos, his Word, his reason; and, in the Holy Spirit, God's power, his wisdom, his truth.

This trinitarian of God has the advantage over all other views of God, in that they are too narrow and incomplete. Lesser views of God convey only the potentiality of divine self-expression and communication. The trinity is our way of confessing our faith in God's many-sidedness without, at the same time, conceptualizing God polytheistically, as pagans, both ancient and modern, always do. The extension of God's being at all levels of his creation can be fully expressed only by reference to the Holy Spirit. The characteristic activity of the Holy Spirit is that it proceeds, or goes out, into creation as God's enabler, as inspiration blowing directly from the mutual relationship and common experience of the Father and the Son.

Black Theology, therefore, if it is to be true to its finest insights and surest revelation, must define the Holy Spirit in terms consistent with our Black theological concept of the holy relational personal God. This "going out" of the Spirit is the divine arising from the intimate personhood and relationality of the holy God, Father and Son, making full the totality of God's being. This same "going out"—in that it extends even as far as to us—is what we mean when we say: "God comes. God has come. God is coming." But it would be better if we were to say: "God is here." God is Holy Spirit at the center of being; God is Holy Spirit present at the center of our being. God does not "come"; he abides, he dwells, he is present. Norman Pittenger called the Holy Spirit the "self expression of God continued, the evidence of God's presence."[12] God's Holy Personhood as Spirit is stable, not intermittent. He is permanently relational, both to the Father and the Son (*ad intra*) and (*ad extra*) to us human beings, not varying. He is intimately indwelling, not an external force or power like some angel or demon or pagan deity or the *loa* of voodoo. The Holy Spirit in the holiness, re-

---

[12]W. Norman Pittenger, *The Word Incarnate* (New York: Nisbet, 1959) 240.

lationality, and personableness of God is, as Bishop Joseph Johnson put it, "the one and only truth from which all other truth is derived."[13] That is to say, it is revelation; it is primordial to our thinking. It is the entrusting by God of his very self to us as the Spirit of Love and Truth. This is why the saints speak of the love of God within them as their own response to God: Spirit communicating with spirit, and spirit responding.

THE CURRENT REALITY OF THE HOLY SPIRIT

In difficult times, the slaves fixed on whatever gave them inner security against the external world; this is still a practical expedient for Black people. The Holy Spirit was the hidden and personal reality who afforded them that security and kept them from total despair. God was with them. That means that the Father and the Son, fused, became available to Black people through the Holy Spirit in their liberation struggles. What God had started with the communicated Word, God continued in the Holy Spirit, becoming even more at one with the human condition of his Black creatures. Whomever God wants to redeem, he becomes at one with. We sang about it all the time in the Spirituals.[14] Perhaps because our situation is not so desperate now as it was when we were in chains, some Black people have lost their sense of God's presence as Holy Spirit. It will take a maturity of faith beyond the views of such new Black theologians as William H. Grier and Price M. Cobbs to perceive the working of the Spirit in our ongoing struggle.

In their two, coauthored books, Cobbs and Grier argue that the "new Black spirit" is the creative response of a tortured, driven people. They see religion as an enslaving force and not as a means of liberation. They conclude that the future of Black people has little to do with Christianity. They do not talk about the work of the Holy Spirit in God's oppressed people.[15]

Perhaps if other Black theologians had done a better job explaining the person and work of the Holy Spirit in the Black experience, neo-Black theologians would not suffer from this spiritual blind-spot. To correct this tendency, I conclude this study with two affirmations: The time has come for Black Theology to develop a full-fledge pneumatology, a Black doctrine of the Spirit, in order to fill out its theological response to the holy personal rela-

---

[13]Joseph A. Johnson, *Proclamation Theology* (published by the author, 1977) 6-7.

[14]Lovell, *Black Song,* chs. 6 and 20.

[15]See Price M. Cobbs and William H. Grier, *Black Rage* (New York: Bantam Books, 1968) and William H. Grier and Price M. Cobbs, *The Jesus Bag* (New York: McGraw-Hill, 1971).

tional God. One good way of doing this is to understand the ongoing work of Jesus Christ eventuating in the Holy Spirit.

Towards a Black Theology of the Holy Spirit

The Holy Spirit is the way that God, in unity with Jesus Christ, has returned and has been with his Black people. Of course, the Spirit of God has been a part of the climate of all human experiences, Black or White, good and bad. But because God is holy, personal, and relational, we identify the Holy Spirit with Black human striving, not with White human oppression. To attain maturity and theological-moral complexity, Black Theology must reflect on the Holy Spirit as central to both that hostile external climate and the spiritual internal reality which have attended Black people in the long liberation struggle. We now live in better times, but the bitter and holy war is not yet over. Black theologians, as prophets of God, must discern the spirits.

The Holy Spirit, as the third person of the Godhead, has been the inward and personal means by which Black people have enjoyed a special identification with God; the spirit has been central to Black people's full awareness of their personhood. Black self-awareness gained refinement and sophistication by relating Black personhood to God the Father and God the Son, conceived in the spiritual unity of God's holy responsive personal being. Therefore, the Holy Spirit is the one who has been and who is still with Black people and available to them in the context of all human conditions in a way similar to the Spirit's holy, personal, and relational unity with the Father and the Son in Godhood. This unity of the human spirit with God's being through God's Spirit, and our awareness of it, has traditionally given Black people the added assurance that God is with them not only in every human condition, but also in a unique and personal way.

In all these ways that God was with us in the past, God is with us yet. Therefore, God is current in his awareness of Black people's special plight. God is still willing to identify fully with his oppressed people; it matters not what they may be! God's current will is to keep on creating his creation through his Word and Spirit. Can we say less than that God is still with us and that God knows what it means to be human?

The unity of God, the Father, with Jesus Christ, the Son, returned to us fused in the Holy Spirit, makes possible our redemption in both a now and not-yet. Belief in the ultimate victory of God's righteousness in this world has always been a source of Black people's hope for Black people's future, no matter what current conditions might prevail. In this hope, Black people have known through faith that God is with them and that God wills fully to meet and overcome all alien powers. This faith-knowledge has been, at times, the only foundation of Black people's hope in Black people's future. Seeing God in this light, God identified with Black suffering, one can understand why Black people of faith have been so certain that God is with them, that God knows their conditions of adversity, and that nothing takes place in their lives without God's knowledge and in which God does not take a hand.

With this knowledge, the Black theologian need never surrender God to evil or make him, to any degree, subject to it. With this knowledge, Black theologians, who have been too silent on the role of the Holy spirit in the Black church and in the liberation struggle, can rediscover the worship of the Black churches; and when the preacher and the worshipers say: "The Holy Spirit is here!" let Black Theology say: "Amen." It was because of this holy visitation that Black people would say, "we have had church." If Black people want to continue to have a church, they had better seek the Holy Spirit to authenticate the presence of God in his visitation.

The Black church has been a Bible-believing church. Black Theology needs to read the New Testament. The synoptic Gospels and John both speak of the "coming one," who would baptize with the Holy Spirit (Mk. 1: 8; John 1: 33; Acts 1: 5). According to Scripture, though Jesus died in shame, he was raised in glory, and is even now with the Father in heaven. God's gift to his followers is the Holy Spirit, who has already begun to transform human beings by giving them a quickened understanding of the Scriptures. The Holy Spirit, then, is our Teacher and our Enlightenment. The Holy Spirit is the one who shares among God's people the broader knowledge and depth of insight into the ways of God in relation to the people of God.

As the Jews taught us, a continuing awareness of God is maintained by a sense of the internal dwelling of the Spirit. This awareness of God inside us lets us know that salvation is not just a saving of the soul alone; it is total salvation. That includes historic deliverance and liberation, like the deliverance of Israel from bondage and their liberation to claim the Land of Promise.[16] The Holy Spirit is still at work, doing the same things, doing something more. The Holy Spirit brings the "age to come" into the "now" of history, transforming and redeeming history itself. Beyond history, the Holy Spirit opens up avenues to sharing God's life after death (Acts 3:15), although life after death was not the main emphasis in the New Testament church. Early Christians were too full of the present gift of God in Jesus Christ and too enthused by the visitation of the Holy Spirit to wonder much about the future.[17] The current reality of the Holy Spirit in the present struggle to liberate life is the properly biblical focus of Black Theology.

---

[16]E. M. B. Green, *The Meaning of Salvation* (Philadelphia: Westminster Press, 1965) 146.

[17]Ibid., 150.

The Holy Spirit was always meant to be and is now an updated enabler, an ongoing teacher, and a progressive means by which we derive more and more awareness of the God-Christ-Spirit fusion within us. Without exception, the Holy Spirit has incited followers of Jesus Christ who understood the work of God in the world to revolutionary actions against this world. The Black awareness of the liberating God is more than affirmation of God's identification with the suffering; it is the assertion of God's active concern and actual participation in the struggle and personal experiencing of the suffering. Suffering has ever moved Christians into the world of action (Acts 8: 4, 17: 6), there to experience and master suffering. Human suffering caused by our fellow human beings has always called Christians to the counterinsurgency of turning the world upside down with acts of mercy and strong deeds of liberation. Ultimate salvation, in the Christian tradition, does not come of God alone; it is a divine-human process or struggle.[18] Salvation is not arbitrary divine action separated from human work, but is achieved as a result of what struggling human beings can do in coaction with God. In this sense, the God of salvation shares with human beings in the mutual struggle for liberation, freedom, and ultimate salvation. It is not enough to say that merely in an inner personal sense, God, through the Holy Spirit, shares with human beings in their struggle with an unsaved self. Rather, God becomes at one with the whole human self in the entire struggle.

In saying this, I am not arguing for a "good works" view of liberation, freedom, and salvation. Paul and other New Testament writers insisted that our response to God in the awareness of the Holy Spirit is a faith-response. Our responses arise together with our faith. Our responses and our faith come to God as through a double door. Faith never is prior to response; without response, there is no faith. Faith is a result of one's personal response to God's initiative in and through the Holy Spirit, and it expresses itself both internally and externally; it is a total response to the total self-giving of God (Eph. 2: 8). Faith, itself, conceived as content, is not the ground on which God accepts us; for then, faith would become a meritorious "work," something of which we could boast as a prior condition before God's initiative.[19]

The task of Black theologians is to develop Black Theology in response to the current life of Black people. To do this, Black theologians need to take seriously the traditional importance of the Holy Spirit for the Black church.

---

[18]Ibid., 151.

[19]Ibid., 169ff. Cf. Oscar Cullman, *Salvation in History,* 323ff. (New York: Harper & Row, 1967). See *The Holy Spirit,* ed. Dow Kirkpatrick (Nashville: Tidings Press, 1974).

Because the Holy Spirit has been the very heart of the Black religious experience since slavery days, to do Black Theology without the Holy spirit is to do theology without the prayer or the worship-life or the heart of Black people. To understand the religious life of Black people is to understand the work of the Holy Spirit; to understand the Holy Spirit is to understand the Afro-American experience of Black people in continuity with the spirit of traditional African religions and the trinitarian Spirit of Christianity.

Above all, Black Theology must proceed to develop its teaching on the Spirit if it is to maintain its voice of moral authority. Our God is a God who gives persons the power to be and to become. The Holy Spirit of God and Christ is the legitimator of Black being at all levels and in all times. Just to be has never been a simple matter for Black people. At times, it has taken more than merely human courage; at times, it has taken sheer tenacity inspired by the Holy Spirit, God's own personal indwelling agent. It was God, and God alone who upheld us; and God is the eternal Creator and Judge, in whose Holy Being rests the total reality of all that is. God's being is the moral law and the ultimate truth on which all human truths, laws, and morality are grounded. But God went to the extent of incarnating himself as communicated Word in crucified human flesh so that love may become known. The Black Messiah was God's greatest expression of love to his oppressed human children. Now, returned to us and fused with Jesus Christ in the Holy Spirit, God binds us to himself and to our fellow human beings with cords of love and mutual respect, opening human eyes to the complete evidence of God as creator and judge, lover and liberator. What God initiated in history through Jesus Christ, God now continues in history, summoning his people to faith through the revelation in Jesus Christ and empowering them to the current work in the Holy Spirit.

The Earthly Life of God in Jesus Christ: Eventuating in the Holy Spirit

The Dutch theologian Edward Schillebeeckx has suggested that only after death can a final assessment be rendered of a person's life. Only after death can one's life be seen as complete, a rounded totality. Consequently, only with Jesus' death does our account begin of who he was.[20] The Black church's Jesus story has always been one about the Son of God who brought us through his person, his preaching, and his way of life and death, the vital message of God's own, unrestricted self-giving love. Without the historical Jesus, God would not be fully revealed. As the Swedish theologian Gustav Aulén wrote,

---

[20]Edward Schillebeeckx, *Jesus: An Experiment in Christology* (New York: Seabury Press, 1979) 404, 603.

"Through historical self-giving, accepted by the Father, Jesus has shown us who God is."[21]

But the Jesus story does not stop with his death, nor does Jesus' revelation of who God is stop at the cross. At one with traditional Christian theology, the Black church has always continued the story by talking about the resurrection, the return to God, and the looked-for coming in glory; but the God-concept prevalent in the Black religious experience called forth a more subjective, a more personal, a more relational account of the continuing life of God in Jesus Christ than merely extending the historical account to include a few more events. The historical Jesus is limited in time and place to history; but the Jesus Christ now fused with God and returned to us in the Holy Spirit is a Jesus Christ who did more than conquer death: He conquers life. When Jesus continues his struggle on the cross and in the suffering of his human condition throughout all history and in our history, there and only then does he become the symbol of God through which we can profoundly relate our struggle, our pain and death, and our life and liberation to God. But Jesus accomplishes his meaning for our life, today, through his fusion with and by eventuating in the Holy Spirit.

The revelation of God's inner nature of love for us made clear in Jesus Christ is kept from becoming blurred by history, because the Holy Spirit keeps Jesus Christ existentially relevant for us, not just an ever dimmer figure from a remote time. Everything that Jesus did and said and was on behalf of God and for our good, he still is and says and does now, today, only more so through the Holy Spirit. God himself, who sometimes seems far away, is brought very near to us in the Holy Spirit.

During the bitter times, the Holy Spirit, God's inner agent—inner to God and inner within us—played the decisive role. It was the Holy Spirit who called, compelled, gathered, restrained, disciplined, and sanctified. It was the Holy Spirit who became our fortress against despair, defeatism, and deep-festering hate. It was the Holy Spirit who first inspired into being the invisible Black Church of Jesus Christ, and then indwelled those Black people of faith and kept the Spirit of Truth about themselves alive within them. It was the holy and personal presence of God's Spirit that affirmed the integrity of Black people's personhood and the legitimacy of their humanity, when the White-controlled churches and the larger society were teaching them the falsehoods of subordination and subjection. And it was—and is—the Holy spirit of everlasting liberty through whom God and Jesus Christ stood in unmitigated

---

[21]Gustav Aulén, *The Faith of the Christian Church* (Philadelphia: Fortress Press, 1960) 221.

opposition against every form and expression of race evil, human disregard, and personal insult. The times are not yet perfect, but they are better because of the work of Jesus Christ and the Holy Spirit. And they will become better yet, as the holy personal relational God continues his uncompromising creation of good and not evil, making love to prevail over fear and hate, and setting at liberty those who were held captive.

Wherever God is at work, he works in and through Jesus Christ and the Holy Spirit. In Jesus Christ, God communicated his Word, the substance of his personal being, and commited thus himself in a relationship to humanity that led him to the cross. This is God revealed to us in active deeds of self-sacrifice on behalf of others—a revelation of godly presence that has continued in our own times. I am thinking about the sacrifice of Dr. Martin Luther King, Jr., who gave his life for others. And there are many more who could be named. In the Holy Spirit, it is the same God doing the same work, working the same deeds of sacrifice and liberation, divine love in the current struggle to set all God's oppressed people free from every form of evil. Therefore, it is the Holy Spirit, fused with Jesus Christ in the Unity of God's being, who reveals to us what God is like.

SUBJECT INDEX

AUTHOR INDEX